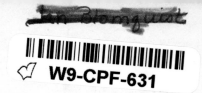

How to Succeed
With Your Children

"The parent is the most important teacher a child will ever have," writes Dr. Harold J. Sala in the early pages of this practical, enlightening book for parents.

To help you meet that awesome responsibility, Dr. Sala has brought together time-honored principles for effective parenting in chapters such as:

- *How to Communicate With Your Offspring*
- *How to Succeed With Your Teenager*
- *How to Discipline Effectively—God's Way*
- *How to Tell Your Children About Sex*
- *How to Convey Values to Your Children*

Put these guidelines to work in your home and you'll find that it still *is* possible—despite the world's mixed-up system of family values—to be a genuine SUCCESS as a parent.

You'll see why God backs up His wise command to "Train up a child in the way he should go . . ." with the beautiful promise: *". . . and when he is old he will not depart from it."*

You'll find new ideas, fresh insights . . . all designed to help you TRAIN UP A CHILD—AND BE GLAD YOU DID.

TRAIN UP A CHILD
AND BE GLAD YOU DID

Harold J. Sala

ACCENT BOOKS
Denver, Colorado

 MEMBER OF
EVANGELICAL CHRISTIAN
PUBLISHERS ASSOCIATION

Second Printing, 1978

Scripture quotations marked NASB are from the New American Standard Bible, © The Lockman Foundation, 1960, 1962, 1963, 1968, 1971, 1972, 1973, 1975, and are used by permission.

ACCENT BOOKS
A division of Accent-B/P Publications, Inc.
12100 W. Sixth Avenue
P.O. Box 15337
Denver, Colorado 80215

Coypright © 1978 Accent-B/P Publications, Inc.
Printed in United States of America

Library of Congress Catalog Card Number: 77-93252

ISBN 0-916406-95-4

To Bonnie, Steven, and Nancy

To the Reader

Being a parent is one of the last hold-outs of the amateurs! To drive a car, operate a CB radio, be a plumber, or practice medicine, you must be licensed—indicating that you have a certain level of training and expertise in performing that function.

But, when it comes to being a parent, no professional training or experience is required. It's easy to *become* a parent, but hard to parent. No wonder Bruce Narramore titled his book, *Help, I'm A Parent!*

Remember the feeling of helplessness you experienced when you first stared into that red, wrinkled little face and realized you had really become a parent? I know I will never forget the emotions I felt as I held my firstborn for the first time and felt so awkward. *What do I do now?* I thought. I still occasionally ask myself the same question—sixteen years later.

The Psalmist wrote, "Lo, children are an heritage of the Lord: and the fruit of the womb is his reward. As arrows are in the hands of a mighty man; so are children of the youth" (Psalms 127:3,4).

Yet, parents today are often sadly wondering whether children are worth it. When newspaper columnist Ann Landers asked her readers whether they would have children if they had it to do over again, 10,000 responded—and 70 percent said *no!* Yet, Solomon wrote of children, "Happy is the man that hath his quiver full of them" (Psalms 127:5). Sorry, Solomon—maybe 3,000 years ago, but not necessarily today.

Something has gone wrong, and that is part of the reason for this book. The teaching and training of children is one of a parent's greatest life responsibilities. If we fail at home, I wonder if we have really succeeded anywhere. Botanist Luther Burbank once said that if we paid no more attention to our flowers than we do to our children, we would soon be living in a jungle.

Years ago Solomon wrote, "Train up a child in the way he should go: and when he is old, he will not depart from it" (Proverbs 22:6). The verb *to train* isn't synonymous with *let them grow up.* It denotes definite direction toward a definite goal. This word is used only three other times in Scripture, and each time it is translated, *to dedicate.* It is the same word used in relation to the temple which Solomon built and dedicated to the Lord.

Your children can learn to love God and grow up with the values you believe in. Don't think for a moment that there *has* to be a period of stubborn rebellion! Parenthood can be an exciting adventure in developing relationships of love and understanding in the family.

May the principles in this book—tested and found solid in the raising of three energetic children in our home—also help you toward that goal.

Contents

1

His Life Is
In Your Hands

1

It's a marvelous thing when God sends a little child into a home! That little bundle of love forever changes your life-style.

A father of three teenagers was thinking just that when he visited a home where a firstborn had just come to live. He pointed to the sleeping little bundle and said, "He looks helpless, but don't be fooled. There lies a potential tyrant. He is plotting right now to run you and this house for the next eighteen years!"

Right from the beginning of parenthood, our lives are forever different—for good or bad, happiness or misery, honor or disgrace, comfort or concern. Once you've become a parent, whether at seventeen or forty-five, you have entered into a new period of existence.

The child who comes into the home may be tiny and helpless—only a babe—but he's a complete person with all the equipment of an adult. He has a mind capable of thinking, a brain capable of reasoning, lungs capable of expressing strong feelings. He has powers of communication, both verbal and non-verbal. He's a full-blown little person, as distinct from everybody else in the world as one snowflake is from another.

As the father of three, I've noticed that our children have distinctly different personalities. Their individual characteristics were evident the first week of their lives. Pediatricians and baby nurses agree that, when a child comes into the world, he is fully equipped to mature into a person different from all the other four billion people on the face of the earth.

At times we are prone to think that a child isn't a real person until he grows out of the preschool state and begins to mature as a child. A four-year-old visited a rather expensive restaurant with his parents. The head waiter handed the little boy a menu and waited a moment before he asked, "And now, son, what would you like this evening?"

Flabbergasted, the boy turned to his mother, "Gee, Mom, he thinks I'm real!"

YOUR OPPORTUNITY AS A PARENT

You can be sure from the beginning, they are real! Whenever I hold a newborn in my arms, I think, "What tremendous potential for good. What an opportunity for a parent to bring out the best in this child." At times, I can't help wondering how history might have been different if one or both parents had given different guidance to some of the children whose names are on the ledgers of history as vile men who plunged the world into war and bloodshed.

From the very beginning, a parent influences a child toward good or evil.

Child-training is an awesome responsibility. J. Wilbur Chapman tells of the time he was standing in Tiffany's in New York and heard the salesman say to a woman, "Madam, this pearl is worth $17,000."

At once, Mr. Chapman was interested. "Let me see the pearl worth $17,000," he said. The salesman put it on a piece of black cloth and Chapman studied it carefully. Then he thought of the tremendous value of Tiffany's inventory. As he looked about the store, he let his imagination wander. He pictured the manager of Tiffany's bringing all their stock to his house and saying, "We want you to take care of this tonight."

What would Chapman do? He would go as quickly as he could to a telephone and ask the Chief of Police in New York City, "I have all of Tiffany's stock in my house, and it is too great a responsibility. Will you send some of your officers to help me protect it?"

"But," continues Chapman, "I have a little boy in my home, and for him I am responsible. If I put all the diamonds and pearls and rubies in the world in one hand, and just put a little boy in the other, the boy would be worth more than all the jewels."

If we would tremble because we had several million dollars' worth of precious gems in our homes for one night, how can we take lightly the responsibility we have for the children in our homes?

That responsibility is made more difficult by the world in which we live. You don't have to be a misty-eyed pessimist to acknowledge that it *is* more of a challenge to raise a child in today's sex-oriented, crime-and-violence-saturated world.

How do you respond to this challenge? Shrug your

shoulders and say, "It's no tougher than when I grew up, and I made it—so they can, too." Or do you say, "I know it's a tough job being a parent, but I'm determined to find God's help in being the mother or father He wants me to be."

By all evidence, the latter is the choice that the Creator of our children would have us make. God is speaking to twentieth-century parents when He says, "Train up a child in the way he should go: and when he is old, he will not depart from it" (Proverbs 22:6).

"IS IT DEAD OR ALIVE?"

Two teenagers decided to play a trick on one of the wise old philosophers who wandered about the Agora, or marketplace, of ancient Greece. One of the boys, they decided, would hold a tiny bird in his hands behind his back where the old man could not see it. Then he would say, "Wise man of Athens, I have in my hands a bird. Tell me, is it dead or is it alive?

If the old man said, "Dead," the boy would open his hands and let the bird fly away, proving the old man wrong. If, on the other hand, he said, "Alive," then *crunch!* The boy would squeeze the little bird to death and then hold it up. So they sought out the wise old man of Athens.

"I have a bird in my hands. Tell us, wise man, is it dead or is it alive?"

A crowd had gathered to see this confrontation of wisdom and foolishness. The old man listened to the question of the boys, thought for a moment, then said, "I don't know whether the bird is dead or alive, but this I know: It's life is in your hands."

What an awesome responsibility—those budding lives in our hands!

Does the Bible give us specific guidance for the task? Does it lay down child-raising principles that we can *really* follow? Does it detail specific responsibilities for parents?

Our world has changed tremendously in the past century, yet the timeless principles contained in the Scriptures are unchanging. Like the old instruction printed on the label, "For best results, follow the directions contained within," God's Word does give guidance—but it is up to each parent to discover these principles and *apply* them.

Obviously, we can ignore them, but we must be willing to accept the results of this kind of disobedience. A mother wanted to impress the visiting clergyman, so she said to her four-year-old, "Now, sweetheart, why don't you run into the bedroom and get God's Book . . . ." The little girl, not knowing what her mother wanted because her mother wasn't accustomed to reading the Bible, replied, "Well, Mom, if it's God's Book, why don't you give it back to Him?" In a real sense, God's Book is a gift to man—His textbook on living. To ignore it is like leaving a beautiful, priceless gift unopened and never realizing the joy found in using it.

BUILD THE FOUNDATION

Throughout *Train Up a Child—And Be Glad You Did* we're going to explore the vital instruction God has given us on effective child-raising and apply it to our home situations. And let's start right now by looking at three very basic guidelines which should be at the foundation of every parent's philosophy.

GUIDELINE ONE: *Realize the training of a child begins at birth and never stops.* For the first eighteen to twenty-one years you are the chief teacher; after that, life takes over. When our third child was born, we brought her home from the hospital and her eight-year-old sister held her in her arms for the first time. Looking down into the wrinkled little face of her baby sister, our little girl observed, "She has a lot of lessons to learn—and I've got just a few." The lessons begin at birth.

The Bible teaches that the training of a child is an *ongoing process* involving the emotional, the physical, and the spiritual. Training involves discipline, guidance, and encouragement.

GUIDELINE TWO: *The parent is the most important teacher a child will ever have.* God instructed ancient Israel to use the home as the classroom where children were first to be taught principles of life and living. Review the great passage found in Deuteronomy, "And Moses called all Israel, and said unto them, Hear, O Israel, the statutes and judgments which I speak in your ears this day, that ye may learn them, and keep, and do them" (Deuteronomy 5:1).

Then Moses gave the Ten Commandments, which were to be moral and spiritual guides to the people. "And these words, which I command thee this day, shall be in thine heart. And thou shalt teach them diligently unto thy children, and shalt talk of them when thou sittest in thine house, and when thou walkest by the way, and when thou liest down, and when thou risest up" (Deuteronomy 6:6,7).

The teaching of the home embraces the whole gamut of life—from worship of God to respect for our elders; from learning to love and respect each member of the family to loving the world about us. We teach by example, through our lives and by the instructions which come from our lips.

GUIDELINE THREE: *Always balance discipline with love.* This is a topic that will be discussed more thoroughly in a later chapter, but keep in mind that *love without discipline is not love,* and *discipline apart from love is only punishment.* Discipline is loving but firm *correction;* it reinforces the total impact of the teaching process. This reinforcement generally results in obedience to the parent, respect for the laws of the land, and a well-ordered personality which can adapt to a given situation.

In the process of trying to raise well-adjusted children whose personalities are not stunted, most parents have become more permissive than they think they should be. At least, that is the result of a survey of 350,000 people published by *Better Homes and Gardens* magazine. An interesting fact about this survey is that most who responded said *they* were not too permissive, but eighty percent of them believed that "most parents" (meaning *other* parents) are too permissive with their children.[1]

Naturally, no one sets out to deliberately ruin his children emotionally and spiritually; nevertheless, it is too often done through parents who neglect to discipline their children. Neglect is indifference, and indifference says to the child, *I don't care enough about you to bother to correct you.*

WHAT KIND OF PICTURE ARE YOU PAINTING?

Whether you realize it or not, your home is a chapel where your child begins to grasp his first spiritual

19

truths. Even Sigmund Freud recognized that Mom and Dad are the first pictures of God to a child.

Perhaps it would be better to say that a mother's and father's love is an expression of God's love to a child. If this is true, what kind of picture of God does your child see in *you?* Psalms 103:13 (NASB) tells us, "Just as a father has compassion on his children, so the Lord has compassion on those who fear Him." Obviously, a father who has no compassion or love for his children can't be the picture of that deeper love—the love of God for His children.

Isaiah 66:13 says, "As one whom his mother comforteth, so I will comfort you . . . ." Here, God points to the love and comfort of a mother as a picture of God's love for us. Mothers, what kind of picture of God are you painting for your children?

Husbands are taught to love their wives as Christ loved the church (Ephesians 5:25). Thus, as children grow up and see the quality of love a husband has for his wife, they develop a picture of Christ's love for all of us.

The message is clear: We are the child's physical model of what God, love and morality are all about. If our example is a shaky one, we can expect from our children little respect for God or our value system. If, however, we totally yield ourselves to God's leading through His Word, our children will see God's love in us and develop a positive view of spiritual and moral truth.

Their lives are in *your* hands, Mom and Dad— from their first moments in the womb until they leave the fold to establish homes of their own. You've been given a crucial job to do. And, as we'll see in the next chapter, it's *never too early* to begin harnessing God's principles of effective parenthood.

2

The Importance
of the
Early Years

2

Occasionally I hear a woman say, "Oh, I don't do anything . . . I'm just a mother."

The woman who says that doesn't realize how very important she is.

Susanna Wesley was the mother of fourteen children, which didn't leave much time for a career outside the home. Her home was her chapel and her great calling in life. History tells us that this busy mother, who didn't have the advantages of push-button laborsaving devices, found time to pray with each child every day and took time to talk to the child individually about his life and spiritual matters.

When Napoleon Bonaparte was asked how to prevent delinquency among youth, he replied, "You begin twenty-one years before he is born by training the grandmother to teach her daughter how to be a real mother."

Winston Churchill, when confronted with an illustrious list of his former teachers, responded

"You have forgotten my greatest teacher—my mother."

The sad letter below appeared in a newspaper:

Today is our son's sixteenth birthday, and it is the saddest day of my life. I just left him in a school for delinquent boys and am heading home, 1600 miles away.

I've had some time to reflect on what went wrong and would like to tell you. My husband and I are hardworking people. I'm a registered nurse. We have five children, and I've always worked to supplement my husband's income. Sunday has always been just another work day for me, so I wasn't a churchgoer. Consequently, our children didn't go either. I see now what a big mistake it was.

Our son began to run with a bad crowd. He did poorly in school. I was too busy to keep an eye on him. His father was not strong enough to discipline him. I knew the boy was drinking, but I couldn't do anything about it. Two weeks ago, the principal telephoned. Our son had been out all night and had come to school Monday morning intoxicated. He was arrested.

So this is the story of a mother's failure. It adds up to no religious training and no discipline in the early years. You have my permission to print my letter if you think it might help someone else.

The letter was signed by a heartbroken mother. The telling sentence bears repeating: "It adds up to no religious training and no discipline in the early years."

Sometimes we refer to the early years of a child as the "formative years." I liken those early years to the launching pad of a great rocket. Picture in your mind the powerful thrust of a Saturn rocket pointed toward the moon 229,000 miles in space. No matter how powerful the rocket, if in its launching it isn't given the right trajectory, it will never hit the target—unless there is a trajectory correction in flight.

We can cry about the accelerating number of crimes committed by juveniles (incidentally, the average age for juvenile crime is constantly lowering), but the real problem is *parental delinquency*. In a very real sense, it is the parents who are responsible for what happens to their child—whether to their glory or disgrace.

In the early years of a child's life, he begins to acquire moral and spiritual values which give definition and meaning to life. Apart from that, there is no moral framework, no ultimate accountability—no reason to be honest, to be responsible, to be respectful. Life becomes a jungle and the law of the jungle becomes, "Do unto others before they get a chance to do it to you."

I can't help thinking of a young mother of four children whose offspring had already had brushes with the law. The older children had been picked up for truancy and minor thefts.

A Christian neighbor had bought clothes for the smaller children and taken them with her to Sunday School. The children complained that their mother wouldn't get out of bed to help them get dressed on Sunday morning. Armed with this knowledge, I decided to pay a visit to the home.

After I had introduced myself, the mother responded, "I don't believe in forcing my children to go to church." She must have felt guilty, because I hadn't even mentioned church. What she really should have said is, "I don't believe in *allowing* my children to go to church."

She continued, "I think religion is a personal matter, and I intend to let my children grow up, then decide if they want any religion."

I paused for a moment, then asked, "Do you force your children to go to school?"

"Yes," she nodded.

"Do you force your children to take baths?"

"Of course!"

"Do you insist that your children take medicine when they are sick? Do you insist that they eat the meals you prepare?"

A forced smile broke across her face as she said, "I see—you've made your point."

But the real point is that we *lead,* not *drive* our children. Our early example is by far the greatest teaching tool at our disposal.

HE'S A QUICK LEARNER . . .

How important are those first three or four years before a baby starts school?

In one word, VERY.

Psychologists tell us that a child gains fifty percent of his knowledge by age three; seventy-five percent by age seven. The young child learns attitudes, responses, character traits. He begins to develop a positive or negative self-image. He learns what he can get away with and where he must stop.

In the early months of a baby's life, he begins to judge how far he can push his parents before they will respond. Before he can talk, he knows how many times Mother will say, "Don't do that," before she reaches over and spanks his chubby little hand.

The child is learning moral and spiritual values as well. Psychologist Paul Wood says, "Unless we imprint the youngster with certain moral standards, by the time he is five or six years of age, we have a task that is extremely difficult."[1]

Dr. James Dobson, author of *Dare to Discipline* and Assistant Professor of Pediatrics at Southern California School of Medicine at Los Angeles, has found that children, even by age three or four, can tell whether other people think they are beautiful or ugly. The beautiful child is praised while the not-so-beautiful child is ridiculed or neglected—the modern version of the ugly duckling. The child without physical beauty is handicapped for life, according to Dobson. He blames a sex-conscious society which puts the emphasis on what a child looks like rather than what he is inside.[2]

What can a parent do to bring out the best in a child? Psychologists are in agreement that a child doesn't wait until his first day of school to begin learning; he starts the day he comes into the world.

The night we brought our firstborn home from the hospital, I learned an important lesson. My wife had almost died in childbirth, and when she and the baby finally came home, it was apparent that I would have to handle the first night shift.

There I was, an awkward young father who didn't know one end of a diaper from another. About ten o'clock the well-meaning relatives left, and I was solely responsible. From ten to midnight, the baby slept—and then she started crying. To save my life I couldn't get her to stop.

I called the hospital, only to hear, "You'll have to wait until morning to contact your doctor." I thought, *I'll never live until then.* But toward the early hours of the morning, I learned my first important lesson as a parent. I discovered that if I held the baby close to me—rather tightly in my arms—she would begin to relax and feel secure. But, if I held her like an awkward bundle of something I could not relate to, she sensed my insecurity and responded by crying.

From the day a child comes into a home, he begins to learn from his parents. Even in the first few months of a child's life, he begins to develop character traits and characteristics that will be with him for life.

In an article entitled, "How Are We Imprinting Our Children?" Dr. S. I. McMillen, a medical doctor, points out that children are like ducklings who learn from their mother. McMillen says that if a mother duck doesn't teach her young to follow her to the water in the first two days, the duckling can be taught to follow any moving object—such as a block of wood. Even more remarkable is the emotional attachment that develops toward that block of wood. If a duckling is that sensitive to a mother's love and direction, how much more is a child impressed by what happens in a home during the early years of his life![3]

. . . AND QUICK TO SPOT A PHONY

A parent should tell his child that he loves him, but the warmth of that love must be *felt,* not just heard. A parent tells his child he loves him by giving of his time, not just his money. A parent tells his child that he believes in truth and honesty and demonstrates by paying the full amount of taxes due the government. He demonstrates that he believes in the civil laws by *following* the speed limit, not simply by *saying* that he believes the laws must be obeyed.

Thomas Harris has authored a best-selling book entitled, *I'm OK—You're OK.* Dr. Harris, who practiced for twenty-five years as a psychiatrist, warns against inconsistent behavior in parents: "When they say, 'don't lie,' and then the child hears them lying, this produces confusion and fear, and the child tries to tune out the discordance." He illustrates the principle with a mathematic equation: "A plus times a minus equals a minus. It does not matter how big the plus was, or how little the minus was. The result is always a minus. The effect in later life may be ambivalence, discord, and despair."[4]

CHILDREN'S RULES FOR PARENTS

We Christian parents are human; we make mistakes, we sometimes fail. But the overall thrust of our life-styles gets through to our children. They know whether we mean business when we pray, "Lord, please forgive me for losing my temper today. I'm sorry. I want to do better." They have a sixth sense that tells them when we are serious or when we are just playing games. A child can spot a phony a mile away.

You may be able to fool your business associates. You may be able to fool your friends and neighbors, but don't think for a moment that you are deceiving your kids. They know you for what you are.

The British psychologist, Dr. R. F. Hertz, conducted a research project of interest to parents. He asked 100,000 children between the ages of 8 and 14 from 24 countries to make a list of rules of behavior for parents. What they said may surprise you:

1. Do not quarrel in front of your children.
2. Don't lie to a child.
3. Always answer children's questions.
4. Treat all your children with equal affection.
5. There must be a mutual tolerance between parents.
6. There should be comradeship between parents and children.
7. Treat your children's friends as welcome visitors.
8. Don't blame or punish your child in the presence of his friends.
9. Concentrate on your child's good points, and don't overemphasize his failings.
10. Be constant in your affection and your moods.

If we analyze these ten points, I think they can be summed up in three words: love, consistency, and acceptance—all mandatory parts of the parents' lifestyle throughout the child's early years. Keep them in the forefront of your mind as we proceed now to study the essential processes of parent-child training—from infancy through the unpredictable, turbulent teen years.

3

How We Teach
Our Children

3

One of our day's most honored musicians is Dr. Suzuki Shinichi of the Matsumoto School in Japan. Dr. Shinichi believes that the early years are the best time to start a child on a musical instrument.

How old are Dr. Shinichi's students? Eight, six, five? No—his method, which has gained world fame as the Suzuki Method, introduces the child to music between the ages of two and four. His theory is that the earlier a child is exposed to music, the better a musician he will become.

As a child imitates the gestures of an adult, he can also learn to imitate the music he hears, believes this accomplished Japanese musician. Dr. Shinichi produces little proteges, barely as tall as their daddy's knees, who play their pint-sized violins like pros.

If the Suzuki method will produce good musicians before the age of six, which is about the traditional age for a youngster to begin school, what could be done by applying the same technique to other areas of life—including the spiritual?

The teaching process developed by Dr. Shinichi involves the parent, regardless of his musical background or the lack of it, who becomes a teacher along with the professional musician. Negatively or positively, a parent is a child's first and most important teacher, molding attitudes, habits, and thought patterns.

We parents teach our children in three ways: first, and perhaps the most basic, is by our example; second, we teach by attitudes, which develop emotional responses in our children; third, by our words.

TEACHING BY EXAMPLE

Many parents seem oblivious to the fact that their example is the greatest force that molds an offspring into the parents' own likeness. That timeworn adage, "Like father—like son," is borne out of the case histories of thousands of behavioral psychologists the world over. However, psychologists say that the son will form the habits of the father *earlier* than his father did.

Watch the little girl as she borrows her mother's old dress and shoes and plays "dress up," and the little boy as he takes his plate and pretends it's a steering wheel. My son was less than a year old when he first took a doughnut, clutched it in both hands, turned it, and made grunting noises. We finally figured out that his doughnut was the steering wheel of the car; his grunting noises, the engine.

Little did one father realize that when he drove

across town commenting on the ability of other drivers, he was also teaching his son. He finally learned what he was doing when someone asked, "Billy, how was the trip?"

The little boy replied, "Fine, but we saw three idiots, four fools, and two blankety-blanks on the road." The father was embarrassed, naturally. He never expected his little boy to give a recital of what he had said, but all the time his words were affecting the impressionable little fellow who sat by his side.

The subtlety of example is that, in most cases, the parent is unaware that a son or daughter is following in his footsteps. The example of adult leadership set before our youth today is, in far too many cases, a deterrent to producing the kind of men and women we want our children to become. The "don't-do-as-I-do, do-as-I-say" syndrome has produced a generation of kids who scream of hypocrisy and label the values of their parents as synthetic and plastic.

Without realizing it, our example frequently teaches a child that honesty and morality are relative—"it's okay, as long as you don't get caught." That's what our example says when we cheat on our taxes and laugh about it, or cruise along the highway at 63 miles per hour, or run the red light when no one (except our kids) is looking. The joke is on the law, but we are teaching our children that authority doesn't really make any difference.

What do politicians teach our young about decency and honesty when high-ranking officials are found to have accepted bribes to vote for or against certain legislation? It's no wonder that kids learn to cheer the bad guy who splits open the head of the dumb cop, and that the boy who cuts in front of a line where fifteen people are patiently waiting is really the good guy because he isn't so dumb as to stand in line like all the rest of the people.

Life today has become infected with a double standard of morality—one that we talk about and want other people to adhere to, and another which we think is okay for ourselves. When we send conflicting messages of verbal honesty and dishonest expample, how can a child have clear standards of what is right and wrong?

A boy consistently had his pencils stolen from his desk at school. "This dumb kid," reasoned the culprit, "can supply all my pencils for me."

When the boy told his father that his pencils were being taken, the father decided he would put a stop to this business once and for all. He marched over to the home of the boy who had taken the pencils.

The conversation went something like this: "I understand that your son has been taking pencils from my son's desk at school and I'm disturbed by this. It is the principle of the thing that bothers me. It isn't the cost—I get the pencils at work. . . ."

Ouch! "I get the pencils at work." Translation: "I steal them from my employer at work—which is okay—but then when your son steals them from my son's desk, that's a different matter."

Living high on expense accounts, keeping duplicate sets of books to beat taxes, making heroes out of underworld characters and heroines out of prostitutes whose memoirs become best-sellers, is projecting a sick, immoral image to kids who are learning by our example day by day and week by week.

Centuries ago, the writer of the book of Judges concluded by saying, ". . . every man did that which was right in his own eyes" (Judges 21:25). Shortly before his death, author John Steinbeck commented on the change in moral climate confronting us today: "I'm not going to preach about any good old days. By our standards of comfort they were pretty awful. What did they have then that we are losing or have lost? Well for one thing, they had rules—rules concerning life, limb, and property; rules governing deportment, manners, conduct; and finally rules defining dishonesty, dishonor, misconduct and crime. The rules were not always obeyed, but they were believed in, and a breaking of the rules was savagely punished."

". . . AS LONG AS NOBODY GETS HURT . . ."

One of the things that bothers me personally is that our present generation of young people have seen such unclear values in the lives of their parents that their consciences have never really been activated. Existential philosophy—the attitude that says, "It's okay to do it as long as nobody gets hurt"— has wiped out the line between right and wrong. A generation is growing up without conscience or a sense of moral caring.

Adlai Stevenson once said of a man, "If he were a bad man I wouldn't be so afraid of him. But this man has no principles. He doesn't know the difference."

The end result is that we are encouraging a generation of men and women to behave almost like animals: pursuing illict sexual fulfillment, looking for success with minimal effort; having no clearly-defined sense of values. The by-products of these attitudes are often anger, distrust, unbridled lust, and overindulgence.

Are we doomed to reap the harvest of our own sowing? Is there any hope for tomorrow? That, of course, depends on what happens in the home. The life conditions in the twentieth century remind me much of the conditions surrounding ancient Israel in the days of the Prophet Jeremiah.

Remember the blunt, outspoken prophet who told of impending doom unless the people turned to God? We today could heed the message of long ago, ". . . Stand ye in the ways, and see, and ask for the old paths, where is the good way, and walk therein, and ye shall find rest for your souls . . ." (Jeremiah 6:16).

But they refused. Again God spoke, ". . . Obey my voice, and I will be your God, and ye shall be my people: and walk ye in all the ways that I have commanded you, that it may be well unto you" (Jeremiah 7:23).

But again, what happened? Jeremiah 7:24 tells us: "But they hearkened not, nor inclined their ear, but walked in the counsels and in the imagination of their evil heart, and went backward, and not forward."

Perhaps the English poet and playwright, T. S. Eliot, was thinking of those words when he spoke of our generation, saying that we are "moving progressively backward." The seeds of moral and spiritual decay have taken root in our way of life. But I'm not willing to write off our generation and the generations to come, to say there is no hope. I believe there is hope, but I am firmly convinced that the *only* hope for the future lies in changed homes charged with the presence of God.

Ask yourself right now, *What am I teaching my child through my example? If my child became more of what I am, would I be pleased or would I try to blame others for what I know I have taught him to do?* Friend, God is still in the business of changing hearts and lives—and He can change *your* life.

TEACHING BY ATTITUDE

Two youngsters are from the same social stratum: Their parents earn approximately the same income; they attend the same school; they may have parents who work side by side. Yet, one child is cautious, hesitant, even fearful, and the other child is confident, aggressive but not pushy, and eager to learn.

Why the difference? One factor may simply be the attitude of the parents. The child may be reflecting the feelings of his parents—whether they are positive and confident, or negative, hesitant and fearful.

Parental attitude follows example as one of the major factors influencing a child. Whether it is good or bad, positive or negative, confident or fearful, enriching or demanding, the attitude of parents shapes the thinking of their offspring. In a sense, the attitude of a parent is an extension of his example.

Attitudes are interesting. The dictionary says that an attitude is *a mental position regarding a given item.* Children often verbalize attitudes when we hadn't really counted on them saying aloud what we had thought. Like the time the patrolman stopped a father. The little boy leaned out the window and said, "Dad, is this one of those stupid jerks you were talking about?" Or a relative comes to visit and your child asks, "Is this that lazy bum who won't work?"

Now the father may not have *said* that all policemen are stupid jerks, but his attitude toward law enforcement—verbal or non-verbal—led his son to believe that. At the same time, you may not have actually said that your brother-in-law is a lazy bum, but you *felt* that way and your attitude left the impression which your child verbalized.

In the insurance business, salesmen talk about PMA—"Positive Mental Attitude." If you have a negative attitude, you convey that attitude to the person you're talking to and will probably lose the sale. But if you're thinking positively, chances are good that your client will catch your enthusiasm and buy the product.

Does attitude make a difference in success or failure? Try knocking on the door of a customer and saying, "You really don't want to buy any brushes, do you?"

CAUTION: ATTITUDES ARE CONTAGIOUS!

Everyday of your life your attitudes are shaping and molding the character of your child. In my dealings with people over the years, I am always amazed at the way grown sons and daughters first get the taste of success as the result of the positive faith placed in them by their parents. Attitudes which make for success rub off.

Show me a parent who is an extrovert, and I can usually show you a son who tends to be an extrovert. Show me a father or mother who is timorous and fearful, expecting the momentary collapse of the world, and I'll show you a son or daughter who is hesitant and lacks confidence. Show me a parent who is generous and liberal in his giving, and I'll show you a teenager who has learned warm-heartedness and generosity because it was practiced at home.

Attitudes are those intangible guides that shape the character and conduct of our children, and one of the disarming things about our attitudes is that we can't fake them. Attitudes are intangible thoughts and concepts that are part of the very atmosphere that permeates our homes.

A mathematics teacher was trying to teach fractions to her pupils. Grasping for an application of the truth she was teaching, she asked the class, "Now suppose that you have six pieces of cake at your house and you have seven people in your family. How much cake would each person receive?"

Immediately a hand shot up. "Yes, Antonio."

"Each of us would have one."

"No, Antonio, that is not correct."

"Oh, yes, because if there were six pieces and seven of us, Mother would say, "I don't care for any—I want each of you to have one." Our children become an extension of our thought patterns and attitudes.

Where does a child first learn about God, love, honesty, decency and character? It is *in the home,* through the lives of his parents.

The Bible says a great deal—both negatively and positively—about our thinking. When the Apostle Paul wrote to the Philippians, he closed by saying, "Finally, brethren, whatever is true, whatever is honorable, whatever is right, whatever is pure, whatever is lovely, whatever is of good repute, if there is any excellence and if anything worthy of praise, let your mind dwell on these things. The things you have learned and received and heard and seen in me, practice these things; and the God of peace shall be with you" (Philippians 4:8,9, NASB).

It's time we parents began conveying some positive mental and spiritual attitudes to which, of course, we must be firmly committed if we are to "sell" our offspring on them. Have you a deeply-settled confidence that God is in charge of the affairs of the world? You may need to get some things settled in your own heart and life before your children can see the confidence you want them to see.

If you are unsure about your relationship with God, it will also be difficult for you to convince your child that "everything works together for good." Parents must realize that when they know Jesus Christ as personal Lord and Saviour, everything is in good hands. You can trust Him to keep Planet Earth moving without your help. Medical doctors tell me that the incidence of ulcers among children age seven through twelve is constantly increasing as we pass on our fears and frustrations to our children.

Have you accepted Jesus Christ as your personal Saviour? Apart from Him, there is little room for optimism and faith. But when you know that you are God's child because Christ has become your Saviour, you need not fear. Faith in God's providence and direction produces a positive mental attitude that stems from a lively confidence in Him who makes no mistake, and neither slumbers nor sleeps.

TEACHING THROUGH OUR WORDS

The telephone rings. Mary answers the phone, and it is for her husband, Bill. She covers the mouthpiece with her hand as she whispers, "Bill, are you here?"

Bill doesn't want to be bothered, so he says, "No, tell him I'm not here—I don't want to talk to him right now."

Three days later, Mary sends her ten-year-old son to the store, and there should be money left over from the items that he is to purchase. When he returns, there isn't much money to give to his mother. "Son, are you sure this is all the money you had left over?"

"Oh, yes, Mother, that's exactly what was left over from the purchase of the groceries."

But what he didn't tell his mother is that he spent part of the money on gum for himself. He looked his mother right in the eye and lied to her. Furthermore, he can lie to his mother and not feel bothered by it at all.

Who taught him that the only important thing is not getting trapped in a lie? You guessed it—his parents. By their example, their attitude, and their words. He concluded that if his parents could tell the truth when it suited their purposes, he could do the same thing.

Centuries ago, God instructed parents—and fathers in particular—that the principles of His Word were to be taught to their children. The passage to which I refer is Deuteronomy, chapter six. Chapter five is a restatement of the Ten Commandments. Then God said, "And these words, which I command thee this day shall be in thine heart. And thou shalt teach them diligently unto thy children . . ." (Deuteronomy 6:6-7).

Did you notice that phrase, "in thine heart"? Perhaps this is the missing ingredient in the lives of many fathers today. Before we can really teach others the importance of honesty, we must have it as part of *our* lives. Otherwise, we send conflicting signals to our children which result in confusion in their lives. We live a double standard, expecting them to be honest when we are not honest with others.

You can encourage your children to be the kind of

persons you want them to become. First, take advantage of your child's questions. "Daddy, why does the butterfly come out of a cocoon? Mommy, how come Uncle Jim went away to Heaven? Daddy, why do I have to brush my teeth?"

THE SOLID INVESTMENT: YOUR TIME

Average parents answer literally dozens—if not hundreds—of questions almost every day covering an array of subjects from sex to Heaven. In some cases, we are so sadly engrossed with our adult activities and responsibilities that we consider the questions of a child an infringement on our time.

It *takes* time to capitalize on the questions of a child, but it pays rich dividends. Educators will tell you that parents who take the time to answer a child's questions are giving him a head start over the child whose parents can't be bothered when it comes to his questions.

The answers to a child's question should be geared to his age and interest span. A six-year-old can't really grasp the principles of an internal combustion engine when he asks, "Daddy, how come cars use gasoline?" But he *can* understand that just as our bodies require food for energy, the car's energy comes from the gasoline that is burned and causes the car to have power. The wise parent, at the same time, is also giving his son a motive for eating all his food.

A parent who will take the time to answer questions can also capitalize on spiritual truth. Don't be afraid that you won't be able to give a proper theological answer, but as you grow in your own understanding of spiritual truth, share it with your child.

A child also learns by the appreciation that is shown by a parent. Years ago, educational psychologist E. L. Thorndike developed a theory of behavior called the "Law of Reinforcement." Simplified, the law states that behavior which is rewarded will tend to recur.

When your pet dog brings a ball to you and relinquishes it, reward him with a piece of meat. Sure enough, after a few sessions, the dog will get the idea that to bring the ball results in a reward. I heard of one fellow who trained a pigeon to examine radio tubes which moved on a conveyor belt—for each successful round, the bird received a piece of grain. I doubt that the labor unions appreciated this, but it does illustrate the Law of Reinforcement.

The principle of praise and appreciation is just the same in the lives of our children. When they do something that pleases us, we need to let them know that what they have done is right and good. This isn't to suggest for a moment that we love our kids only when they are good. But it *does* mean that we realize our children are human beings who respond to appreciation and praise just as adults do. Dr. James Dobson applies the same principle when teaching a child to assume responsibility. When a youngster assumes responsibility, he should be rewarded; when he fails to carry out his assigned tasks, he should be penalized.

Finally, I would suggest that we teach our children sportsmanship and values as we play with them. I know a teenager who was apprehended for stealing an automobile. He had grown up in the asphalt jungles of the big city, with no father. His toys were the garbage pail lids and sticks that were found in the streets. When he was sent to a rehabilitation center operated by Teen Challenge, he not only saw his first green field and heard for the first time that God loved him and that his life could be different, but he also experienced what it was like to feel the sweat of good, clean competition—not the sordid thrill of hitting someone and fleeing through a dark alley.

Sportsmanship and principles of fair play can be taught as we take time out from our busy schedules to play with our families. This is one of the reasons that I'm a big believer in family recreation. It's great to spend time together outdoors whether you camp, fish, or simply walk through the woods or along a beach.

Perhaps you live in a large city where transportation is difficult, but you can still learn to play together—whether it is dominoes or chess—and you can demonstrate how to lose graciously, as well as how to play hard to win.

Teaching: It goes on all the time by our example, our attitudes, and our words.

4

Learning to Communicate with Your Offspring

4

The process of parent-child communication actually begins before birth as a mother communicates warmth and security to an unborn child. From the day of his birth, a child quickly learns to communicate with a world that seems hostile to his existence. When he's hungry, he yells. When he feels pain or discomfort, he screams again.

Soon, a baby communicates with laughing eyes and fat little dimples. He giggles and warms everyone's heart. Parents begin to communicate, too. A baby who is held firmly feels secure and soon senses, through physical contact, what love is. From the beginning, he's a complete human being— undeveloped, untrained, an unknown quality, but he's all there—a real person. What he becomes is, in a real sense, up to the parents.

As the child begins growing from infancy to adolescence, there are two other basic ways parents communicate with him. First, as we saw in the previous chapter, *we communicate by the example of our lives.* The conscious effort of little children to mimic their parents in play is an indication that the life-style of a parent has gotten through. It's kind of a miniature playback of what the child sees. I don't know whom to credit with these lines, but I do know that what the author wrote is 100% accurate:

> If a child lives with criticism,
>   He learns to condemn.
> If a child lives with hostility,
>   He learns to fight.
> If a child lives with ridicule,
>   He learns to be shy.
> If a child lives with shame,
>   He learns to feel guilty.

> If a child lives with tolerance,
>   He learns to be patient.
> If a child lives with encouragement,
>   He learns confidence.
> If a child lives with praise,
>   He learns to appreciate.
> If a child lives with fairness,
>   He learns justice.

> If a child lives with security,
>   He learns to have faith.
> If a child lives with approval,
>   He learns to like himself.
> If a child lives with acceptance and
>   friendship,
> He learns to find love in the world.

Second, *we communicate by the verbal teaching-learning process*. The parent is the child's first great teacher. In communicating with our children, there are several things to remember if we are to be effective. We must remember our age and the age of this little pint-sized enigma who fires questions faster than we can put down the newspaper to respond.

A few days ago I was visiting in the home of a brilliant scientist. He has an inquisitive four-year-old girl who seemed to ask a question every third time she inhaled. That bounding little dynamo of energy would say, "Daddy, why is this and why is that...?" As I listened to the explanations offered by the scientist, *I* hardly understood them. How could a four-year-old?

Answer a child's questions in simple *child's* language. Every "Why?" from a child doesn't demand an explanation. Children must learn obedience apart from a lengthy explanation of why a child is to drink his milk or why he has to take a bath. But the sincere questions of a child offer tremendous opportunities for communicating knowledge and truth.

TROY REVISITED

When Robert Browning was five, he saw his father reading a book and asked, "What are you reading about?" A lot of fathers would have pushed the question aside with the casual answer, "A book— now don't bother me, Son." But not the father of Robert Browning! Looking up from his book, the father said, *"The Siege of Troy* by Homer."

"What is Troy?" asked little Robert.

Two questions in a row, and what would the

average father do? He'd probably reply "A city in Asia; now, no more questions." But not Robert Browning's father! He put down the book and said, "Let me show you."

There in the living room he built a city of tables and chairs. On top of one table he put an armchair for a throne and popped little Robert into it. "There now," he said, "that's Troy and you're King Priam, and—let me see—here's Helen of Troy, beautiful and sleek," and he pointed to the cat near the footstool.

"Outside—you know, the big dogs in the yard always trying to get inside—they are the fighting kings, Agamemnon and Menelaus, and they are making a siege of Troy so as to capture Helen." And he told the story in terms a five-year-old could understand.

Later, when Robert was seven or eight, his father gave him a translation of the *Iliad* to read, encouraging him to start it in Greek. By capitalizing on the boy's questions and readiness to learn, Browning's father was able to teach him Greek and poetry, as well as an energetic attitude toward life's problems.

God places the responsibility of teaching a child squarely on the shoulders of a parent. Moses commanded that parents should teach their young, saying, "And these words . . . thou shalt teach them diligently unto thy children, and shalt talk of them when thou sittest in thine house, and when thou walkest by the way, and when thou liest down and when thou risest up" (Deuteronomy 6:6,7). The Bible also tells us that the questions which come from a child are great opportunities for teaching spiritual truth.

Remember how Joshua instructed the Israelites to

place twelve stones from the midst of the Jordan River on the shore so that when subsequent generations asked, "What do these stones mean?" the fathers could explain the miracle of God in stopping the waters? Parents are always teaching—yes, communicating—with their children. Beat them, coddle them, ignore them, worry about them, love them or hate them—parents are sending messages to the child.

The father who says only "hello" to his son and heads for the easy chair is communicating in a negative fashion. He's telling his child that he doesn't rate the time and energy it takes to sit down and play a game with him, or toss a ball, or plan a fishing trip together.

If you have a little child who is full of questions and you grow weary, you may not have the energy to answer right then. But you can reply, "Son, Mother or Daddy is very tired right now. Ask me in the morning, and I'll explain it to you." That communicates your interest in the child and his question, but it also lets him know that you have needs in your life which also have to be met. Remember your age and his. The world doesn't revolve around a five-year-old. He must learn to fit into the overall structure of the family. Child-raising is the raising of a child by parents—not the raising of parents by a child.

COMMUNICATING WITH TEENS

When the Apostle Paul wrote to the church of Rome many years ago, he said that we are one body but individually members one of another (Romans 12:5). The same thing is true of the family unit. Unique individuals make up the whole, yet we are part each of the other, and when one member suffers, the entire body suffers.

I know something of the anguish that comes to the parents of a teenager who repudiates everything a parent has taught and brings disgrace to the family name. I've agonized with parents who searched for a girl or a boy who had slipped out of their lives into the night. But the teen didn't slip out of the hearts and lives of the family quite so easily. A few postcards with no return address read, "Don't worry about me. I'm okay." But parents *do* worry, and the unanswered questions etch creases in the forehead and put gray in the hair.

Several years ago, a young woman was one of several youths who murdered a pregnant movie star and her companions in a bloody, ritualistic killing that attracted worldwide notoriety. When she was brought to trial, reporters asked her father if he would stand by her during the trial. Her father told newsmen, "I don't know how to stand by her—I lost her." Many a young woman doesn't end up on trial for murder but the statement of the father is exactly the same, "I don't know how to stand by her—I lost her."

What can we do to keep the lines of communication open between parents and teens? If communication ceases between a parent or a set of parents and their teenager, *something has happened to interrupt the process of communication!*

A youth becomes a teenager one day at a time. The normal pattern is for the process of communicating and sharing our lives one day at a time to continue throughout life. My point is that somewhere communication is broken, even though the break may take place very gradually.

Contrary to popular opinion, one survey conducted among hundreds of teens from various backgrounds revealed that the majority of teenagers between the ages of 13 and 18 feel they *can* talk over serious problems with their parents and they *do.* Many of them feel, though, that parents don't understand the world they live in, and that their own peers understand their feelings better than parents do. They have a point. A fifteen-year-old can perhaps understand how another fifteen-year-old feels better than his forty-year-old mother can, but what the fifteen-year-old lacks is twenty-five years of experience.

When a communication gap exists, we parents may have created the gap by inadvertently moving away from our teens' needs. Perhaps we unknowingly closed the door to communication through responses as diverse as indifference and open hostility. There's a better way.

Stay close to a teen by spending time with that youngster. My beard isn't gray and my hair hasn't completely fallen out, but I've been around long enough to observe that the families that have the biggest generation gaps are the ones that have had little discipline and little recreation together as a family.

Another observation based on experience: The families that have never heard of generation gaps are usually the ones where other teens are welcome. There may be anywhere from one to a half-dozen extra plates for dinner even though guests weren't invited—and no one worries about it. The child's friends happened to be there, and the food was shared. The no-problem-communicating families are the ones that don't mind a few pop bottles on the coffee table or a few crumbs on the furniture. They're also the ones who know where a son or daughter is and can tell you when he will arrive home just about to the minute. It isn't by chance that some families stay close to each other and others drift apart.

SUCCESS STARTS AT THE DIAPER STAGE

The way to eliminate communication problems with teens is to start when they are in diapers, by guiding them with a firm, loving hand—and then staying close together as they reach their teen years. The rebellious teen who's on the other side of a generation gap may not realize it, but he has a deep resentment for the lack of guidance and discipline in his life.

Here are three money-back guaranteed guidelines for communicating with your teens.

GUIDELINE ONE: *Accept your son or daughter as a young man or woman who's in the process of becoming.* He hasn't arrived. He's a philosopher, idealist, pragmatist, liberal, conservative, artist, poet, critic—all at the same time. He's aggressive at times, shy at others, and a paragon of virtue—simultaneously. He's a walking contradiction of ideas and thoughts; he's awkward physically and often lacks confidence, but he's the young man or woman who's in the process of becoming an adult.

That's why a teen needs clear, definite guidance, with few sermons and little criticism. He needs models—parents who can show him better ways—without feeling that he is being attacked or labeled as stupid or rebellious because he expresses ideas without thinking through the implications.

If more parents would remember the wild, crazy ideas they had between fifteen and twenty, they could perhaps have more understanding about some of the rather absurd-sounding thoughts their children have.

GUIDELINE TWO: *Family recreation is a great aid to communication.* What can families do together? Hike, bike, walk, play tennis, camp out, shoot, fish, hunt, sail, go to the beach or to the mountains.

I know what you're thinking: *That sounds good if you have a lot of money, but we just don't have the money for recreation equipment.* I've got good news for you. Recreation takes energy, but recreation can be geared to the budget of your family. There are some things you can't afford to do, and there are other things you can't afford not to do.

When a teen gets into trouble, our value system changes almost overnight. The father who hasn't had time to do anything now has time to go to court, to talk to a judge and take a boy for counseling. There's been no money for recreation equipment, but now there's money for professional help which wouldn't have been necessary had he only taken time and spent what he couldn't afford not to spend. You don't have to always go first class, but you can have first class fun with what you have. Try purchasing used sports equipment and upgrade as the budget allows, but don't think that you can't do anything because you don't have the money.

GUIDELINE THREE: *Pray together as a family.* Have you heard the old adage, "The family that plays and prays together, stays together"? Many young people today are in the firm grip of a pessimism that says there is nothing to live for, that all there is to life is the pleasure of living *this very moment.* One teenager wrote, "Our generation knows that a wrong finger on the right trigger could blow up the world. So we live for today 'cause tomorrow may never come."

Faith in God eliminates the pessimism and grim fatalism that cries, "Stop the world; I want to get off!" Prayer is a link that gives meaning and purpose to life. It has a way of bringing families together. The richness of faith in God and His wise providence makes a difference in the lives of men and women. Illicit sex, drugs, rebellion, even violence, are side effects of a generation seeking answers.

THE ATMOSPHERE OF YOUR HOME

We aren't expected to let our neighbors know that Christ is the head of our home by hanging a sign on the mailbox, *God lives here!* But in addition to the *social* atmosphere of the home, there can be physical evidences of Christ's headship that will serve as a constant testimonial to your children, neighbors and friends.

G. Campbell Morgan, the great British expositor of the Bible, once told how his father came into his home after he was married and looked around in every room, then said, "Yes, it is very nice, but nobody will know, walking through here, whether you belong to God or the devil."

Morgan said, "I went through and looked at the rooms again, and I thought: He is right. So we made up our minds straightway that there should be no room in our house, henceforth, that had not some message, by picture or wall text, for every corner should tell that we serve the King." That was one way that the Morgans announced to the world that

God was at home in their house.

There is a Biblical basis for what he did. It is found in Deuteronomy, when God instructed that the words which He gave should be in the hearts of the Israelites and that they should be taught to the children. And then God commanded, "And thou shalt write them upon the posts of thy house, and on thy gates" (Deuteronomy 6:9).

The timeless principles of God's Word know neither age nor decay. God says that the atmosphere of your home is important in communicating Biblical principles to your children. Does it make any difference whether your home is identified as a Christian home?

We are bombarded by sensory stimuli today! Everywhere we turn we receive messages that we ought to buy this toothpaste or that deodorant. We are even told that one particular automobile has "sex appeal" (if such a thing is possible). We are very much guided—often in very subconscious ways— in our purchasing by what we have seen and heard in the mass media.

The same is true in our homes. My grandmother is in Heaven, but I will never forget some of the Scripture mottos which hung in her humble home. One which must have been at least a half-century old was a folded, dingy banner, but the message endures: "The Lord is my Shepherd, I shall not want . . . ."

In *The Christian Family,* Larry Christenson tells of a woman whose three sons, to her great disappointment, all took up the life of seafaring men. One day she was telling a friend in her home how disappointed she was that all three boys had gone to sea, and that she couldn't understand why they had done this.

"How long have you had that picture?" the visitor inquired, pointing to a large painting that hung in the dining room.

"Oh, for years," the woman replied, "ever since the children were small."

"There is your answer," the visitor said. In the picture, a large sailing vessel cut smartly through the waves, its sails at full billow. The captain stood straddle-legged on the quarterdeck, his spyglass in hand, scanning the horizon. Morning, noon, and night—with every meal—the boys had taken into their inner consciousness the sense of high adventure portrayed in that picture. Effortlessly, with never a word being spoken, it had planted in them a hankering for the sea.[1]

I am fully aware that no one today knows what Christ really looks like, but a picture of Warren Sallman's head of Christ which has hung in our living room for years lets people know immediately that God is at home in our house. On many occasions, the painting has given us the opportunity of telling about our faith and trust in the Lord.

A VISIBLE WITNESS

Take inventory of your home. Is there anything in your home to suggest God is at home there? That Christ is a risen Saviour? That you believe in the power of prayer? And that you believe the Bible is the Word of God?

In the last few years the hobby of decoupage has brought all kinds of crafts and wall decorations within easy reach of the budget of the average person. Take a simple card with a message on it and presto, it's attached to a board with a glaze of decoupage that makes it look as nice as anything done professionally. A visit to a Christian bookstore or church store in your area may help you tell the world that God is at home in your house.

I know that what really counts is what happens in your heart and life—not just the message that you put on the wall—but I'm also aware that identifying yourselves as Bible-believing men and women helps your kids grow up with the positive message that Mom and Dad know where they stand in relationship to God. The physical atmosphere of your home is as much a part of good communication with your children as the social atmosphere.

A few days ago I was in a home and was asked to say hello to a teenage boy who lived there. As I went into his room, it took my eyes a while to grow accustomed to the purple glare from the black light which illuminated the room. On the wall were psychedelic posters of his heroes—bearded, leather-jacketed young rebels with dark glasses. Other lights flashed on and off to the sound of rancorous music blaring from a stereo system.

I couldn't help wondering what five or six hours—let alone several years of the combination of distorted rock music, flashing lights and psychedelic art would do to the mind of an impressionable youth. No, I really didn't have to wonder. I *know* what it does. The constant distortion of music and light gradually produces a distortion of mind and body because you become what you see, what you hear, and what you think.

The Bible tells us that "As a man thinketh in his heart, so is he" (Proverbs 23:7). Your son or daughter is your responsibility, and what goes on in his or her room and goes up on the walls is also your responsibility. The atmosphere of your home is part of your witness and testimony. It is also one of the ways that we parents help our children communicate with God.

When one California church built a new building, they decided to let the high schoolers choose the colors of their rooms and decorate them appropriately with minimal guidance from the adult teaching staff. One high school class wanted to have a clear witness of what they believed, so they painted one wall . . . pastel white? Not on your life! Light yellow? Wrong again. Brilliant lavender! And in the center a budding artist painted the words, "JESUS POWER!" with beautiful scroll work around the letters. It hurt the eyes of a few old-timers, but soon everybody wanted to see that room.

After taking inventory, you may want to do some redecorating to let the world know that God is at home where you live.

5

How to Discipline
God's Way

5

Newspaper columnist Ann Landers tells of the time that she witnessed an argument between an eleven-year-old boy and his mother. The boy wanted a piece of cake; Mom said he couldn't have it. But the boy wasn't about to take "no" for an answer, and became louder and increasingly abusive to his mother.

Finally the child shouted, "You go to hell!" as he grabbed the piece of cake and ran out of the room. The mother turned to Ann Landers and said, "He's going through a phase and it requires enormous maturity on my part not to show anger when he gets like that. It's a real challenge to raise a child these days when the kids are so smart. Do you agree?"[1]

Ann Landers *didn't* agree with any theory of child raising which refuses to recognize the importance of discipline. "In my opinion," wrote the columnist, "the theory of permissive upbringing is the most damaging concept ever latched onto by a generation of mixed-up parents. It has produced a shocking number of disturbed and spoiled brats. Remove the rose-colored glasses, folks. They contain no correction for parental myopia."[2]

For about three decades a host of parents have raised their children with permissiveness, having been told that to discipline a child will repress his personality. The result: Juvenile delinquency is at an all-time high, while respect for authority is at an all-time low. Since World War II, we have seen the greatest acceleration of crime and offenses against school property in the history of education. Acts of violence by teenagers toward other students, teachers, policemen and government officials are rampant.

It is little wonder that in recent years behavioral psychologists have begun to call for a return to "old-fashioned" principles of discipline as part of the teaching-training process so sadly neglected by many adherents of "progressive" education.

"For a long time," says Dr. Edward Litin, chairman of the department of psychiatry at the Mayo Clinic, "parents have been afraid to say no, afraid to give orders, afraid to punish their children, because they fear the loss of the child's love." But many psychologists have come to reject the permissive view. "Discipline and love," says Dr. James Dobson, "are not antithetical. One is a function of the other."[3]

Dr. William Glasser, the psychiatrist who pioneered an approach to psychiatry called "reality therapy," says, "The responsible parent . . . teaches [his child] responsibility through the proper combination of love and discipline. . . . People who are not at some time in their lives, preferably early, exposed intimately to others who care enough about them both to love and discipline them will not learn to be responsible. For that failure they suffer all their lives."[4]

CAN LOVE BE WITHOUT DISCIPLINE?

Discipline is very much a part of love. While you can discipline your child without loving him (which is probably really just punishment), it is questionable that you can really love him without disciplining him.

Although discipline as part of child-raising is relatively new to contemporary psychology, it is actually a very old concept. Centuries ago, a writer of Scripture declared that discipline is the result of real parental love, just as God's discipline for His children is the result of His love and concern for our lives.

"My son," wrote Solomon, "do not reject the discipline of the Lord, Or loathe His reproof, For whom the Lord loves He reproves, Even as a father, the son in whom he delights" (Proverbs 3:11,12, NASB).

In the New Testament, this thought is amplified: "My son, do not regard lightly the discipline of the Lord, Nor faint when you are reproved by Him; For those whom the Lord loves He disciplines, And He scourges every son whom He receives" (Hebrews 12:5,6, NASB).

Our English word, *discipline,* comes from the Latin, *discere,* which means "to learn." The Bible consistently pictures discipline as the great reinforcer of the teaching-learning process. Consider some of the following references to the importance of discipline and its part in raising children:

> "Discipline your son while there is hope, And do not desire his death" (Proverbs 19:18, NASB).
>
> "Whoever loves discipline loves knowledge, But he who hates reproof is stupid" (Proverbs 12:1, NASB).
>
> "Stern discipline is for him who forsakes the way; He who hates reproof will die" (Proverbs 15:10, NASB).
>
> "He who spares his rod hates his son, But he who loves him disciplines him diligently" (Proverbs 13:24, NASB).
>
> "And fathers, do not provoke your children to anger; but bring them up in the discipline and instruction of the Lord" (Ephesians 6:4, NASB).

Discipline did not originate with parents who needed a way to vent their anger and frustration on their kids. It began with God, who gave us the concept as part of His plan to help our children grow up to be well-adjusted men and women respecting their parents and the established order of their society. God instructed parents—fathers in particular—to discipline their children in order to save heartbreak and anguish. A host of parents today could testify to untold hours of suffering that could have been avoided had they only learned the importance of discipline.

One mother, having heard my radio program, wrote telling about a daughter who had been raised with little, if any, discipline. Today the daughter has no respect for her mother, and having rejected conventional morality, is living with a man to whom she is not married. "I had prayed for a daughter before she was born," wrote the mother, "but I never dreamed of the shame she would bring to us now."

WHAT DOES DISCIPLINE ACCOMPLISH?

Discipline produces happy, well-adjusted children. An undisciplined child is never a happy youngster. To the contrary, he's frustrated, sulky, and just plain spoiled. He becomes an angry little tyrant who gets his way by throwing a fit or anything else that is handy.

Ethel Barrett encountered such a youngster in a beauty shop, where a four-year-old boy started screaming like a renegade on the warpath. After a few moments, a gray-haired lady gruffly barked, "Sit down!"

He didn't. Instead he picked up a magazine and hurled it at her.

She repeated the order, "Sit down!" But this time, she picked him up and popped him into a chair. Grossly offended, the youngster let out a howl loud enough to bring the police, so she picked up the magazine he had thrown at her and began to leaf through the pages. "What's that?" she asked, pointing at a picture. The boy ignored her, still screaming at the top of his lungs.

She turned page after page, calling the boy's attention to the pictures until his temper had subsided and he was calmly naming things on the pages. The child wiped away his tears and sat there quite contented, when it was the lady's turn to have her hair done.

"Now you sit here and look at this magazine," she instructed, and this time he did. As Ethel Barrett passed by, she said, "My, you have an intelligent child."

"My child?" responded the woman. "Why, I never saw that kid before. I saw that he needed discipline and decided to give it to him."

"All discipline for the moment seems not to be joyful, but sorrowful; yet to those who have been trained by it, afterwards it yields the peaceful fruit of righteousness" (Hebrews 12:11, NASB).

Discipline produces a security that draws the limits on behavior. It eliminates the frustration that comes to a child who doesn't know what is acceptable and what is taboo. "Children feel more secure," says Dr. Haim Ginott, author of *Between Parent and Child,* "when they know the borders of permissible action."[5]

Some of the largest cattle ranches in the world are found in the state of Texas. If you should go to the largest ranch there and ask the foreman to show you the boundaries of the property, he would probably take you miles and miles from nowhere. When you got there, you would probably find at least one cow trying to reach the grass on the other side of the fence. Not content to graze on the thousands and thousands of square miles which are easily reached, that cow will try to go just a little further than the limits allow.

By nature, we humans do the same thing. Wherever the line is drawn, we will try to push it just a little further. And by no means are our children an exception.

"Be in by 10:30."

"Aw, Mom, can't I stay out 'til 11?"

If your offspring learns that 10:30 *means* 10:30 and not 10:50, he will be a better-adjusted youth. Indefinite boundaries and inconsistent standards produce an insecurity that further causes kids to ignore any standard a parent may try to set. Indefinite limitations—poorly defined and enforced—also result in an emotional instability where life itself is not clearly defined.

Discipline produces obedience. Jesus Christ, you will remember, grew up in the framework of a family with brothers and sisters who filled the carpenter shop and ran and played in the streets and fields of Nazareth. Yet, in spite of having the knowledge that His mission and purpose were different from those of the rest of the members of His family, Jesus still submitted Himself to the discipline of Mary and Joseph and "was obedient to them" (Luke 2:51).

Speaking of a greater discipline—the result of what Christ had first learned in the home—the writer of Scripture later says, "Though he were a Son, yet learned he obedience by the things which he suffered" (Hebrews 5:8).

David Wilkerson, founder of Teen Challenge, believes that a large percentage of young people who are on drugs today have taken that path as the result of having been raised in permissive homes where parents have failed to set standards and adhere to them.

Many parents say, "Don't do that!" and they don't mean it. Their kids *know* they don't mean it. And when the parent says, "If you do that, I'll . . ." their kids further know, when it comes down to it, that the parent won't back up *that* statement either. Why comply? They've learned, through the parent's inconsistency in follow-through, that if they defy the order, the parent will back down. Appeasement *never* produces obedience!

How much different might our generation of youth be if they had grown up in homes where parents meant business when they said, "If you do this, I'll . . . ." At least one parent has made a believer out of his son—one of those perfectly normal little boys who went to bed and just couldn't stay there. Whether his nap was too long, or he just couldn't get to sleep, going to bed at night had become a kind of game. One night, after the father had tucked the boy into bed about the fifth time, he said, "Now, Son, if you get out of bed one more time, or if you say one more word, I'm going to spank you. Do you understand?"

"Yes, Daddy," the little guy replied.

But just a few restless moments later, the boy's mouth was again as dry as cotton. He knew he'd already had a couple of drinks, two songs, three goodnight kisses, and one trip to the bathroom. He'd also received one of those "I-mean-business-when-I-tell-you-I'm-gonna-spank-you" talks from a daddy who kept his promises.

He tossed and turned, but he couldn't take it any longer. "Daddy?"

"Son, you know what I told you!"

"Yes, Daddy, but when you get up to spank me, will you please bring me a glass of water?"

Discipline provides guidance until a child is capable of reasoned value decisions. Before a child can understand the reason behind something, he must learn to obey simply because a parent has asked him to. Responding immediately to the instruction of a parent has on more than one occasion saved the life of a child.

About the age of three, most normal children get into the habit of saying, "Why? Why do I have to?" And a lot of parents fall into the trap of responding with adult-sized explanations which the youngster can't grasp. One pint-sized small fry asked, "Why?" and his father gave him a three-minute explanation which his son didn't understand. Again, the kid barked, "Why?" this time a little louder and more defiantly, whereupon the father (slightly burned) said, *"BECAUSE!"*

"Okay, Daddy," said the boy and he did it. Don't fall into the trap of offering an explanation every time you give your child instructions. Remember that discipline produces obedience which results in a well-integrated personality.

Discipline enables a child to assume responsibility. Dr. William Glasser writes, "Parents who are willing to suffer the pain of the child's intense anger by firmly holding him to the responsible course are teaching him a lesson that will help him all his life. Parents who do not do so are setting the pattern for future irresponsibility. . . ."[6]

Seldom if ever do you find a boy from a disciplined home who can't hold a job because he oversleeps or can't be depended upon, who is convinced that the world owes him a living and he's out to collect. Seldom does a young man lack opportunity who has grown up in a home where discipline is practiced. He succeeds because he's dependable and consistent and can accept responsibility.

Think of some of the great men of history—men who made their mark in life—and you will find that one of the common qualities that made them successful was their ability to discipline themselves, a trait that was learned as the result of being disciplined as a child.

TEN GUIDELINES FOR SUCCESS-FUL DISCIPLINE

GUIDELINE ONE: *Establish clear limits of behavior.* Dr. Haim Ginott says children "need a definition that tells them clearly what constitutes unacceptable conduct and what substitute will be accepted. The limit must be stated firmly so that it carries only one message. 'This prohibition is for real. I mean business.'"[7]

When you say, *"No, you can't do that"* one day and turn around and let your child get by with it the next day, then punish him for the same thing a day or two later, how will he really know what constitutes acceptable behavior and what will not be allowed?

If you tell your children, "Absolutely no eating in the living room" but lower your resistance when you are tired to "I guess it's okay today," you are sending a conflicting message to your child: *Sometimes yes, sometimes no—depends on my feelings!* This is confusing to a child and the result is that he will do whatever he wants and feel that you are unfair when you punish him for what is allowed at other times.

Children are born with an amazing sense of radar and can usually read your emotions quite well, but consistency eliminates confusion. On the other hand, if you allow yourself to get into the habit of not meaning business until you have raised your voice to a certain level, you can be sure that nothing you say will register until you get loud enough or tense enough.

On one occasion, I had dinner with a family whose little darling decided she would rather throw her food than eat it. The first time she flung a handful of peas across the table, her father said, "Now, if you do that one more time, I'm going to spank you."

What happened? A repeat performance, followed by a second warning: "Now, if you do that one more time, I'm going to spank you."

Third demonstration, third warning. Fourth demonstration, fourth warning.

Finally, he picked up the little girl and took her to another room and spanked her. After a few minutes the girl was brought back to the table where she sat and ate her meal like a little angel.

That girl had learned that it didn't mean a thing when her daddy said, "If you do that one more time, I'm going to spank you," and she took full advantage of the situation.

How many times should a child be warned before he is disciplined? *Only once*—to clarify the boundaries of unacceptable behavior. After that, you had better mean business.

You may have to fight the temptation to let your voice rise with your emotions, but don't do it! Your kids will quickly get the message that what Mom or Dad says is for real if you make it a practice to speak only once for clarification: "We aren't going to put up with that, and I mean business." Then, follow through.

GUIDELINE TWO: *Enforce boundaries with consistent discipline*. It is at this point that parents either hang together or hang separately. If you and your mate cannot agree on discipline, your children will quickly realize it and play you both against each other.

"Dear Dr. Sala," wrote one parent, "my wife and I have had a disagreement on discipline for the past thirty years, and it's too late now, but I'd like to have your message dealing with this idea of discipline.... In a few years when our youngest, thirteen years old, is through her high school, I'm planning on leaving since my responsibility is complete." In that home the failure to agree on principles of discipline constituted a divisive problem that pitted a husband and wife against each other.

"Divide and conquer" is the old cliche applicable to warfare *and* to parents who can't agree on discipline. A general principle to follow is: Once either parent has laid down a supreme court ruling when it comes to what a child can or cannot do, the other parent had better back him up 100 percent or trouble is sure to follow.

If parents have a loose chink in their armor, their children will find it every time and play one parent against the other. It can be devastating. If a mother has a question as to what should be done, she can always say, "Let me talk this over with your father and we will let you know," or vice versa. But once one parent has said, "No," and the other says, "Okay," you can be sure that the child will do what he wants to do and the authority of both parents has been undermined.

I suggest that if your mate makes a decision and you disagree, support him in the decision and then talk it out privately—out of the hearing of your children. To come up with a split opinion not only hurts your child, but your relationship with your mate.

In an age of overindulgent, tired, and pressured parents who sometimes don't have the mental energy to put their foot down, we need to learn the power of the positive "No!" Let's face it—it is often "easier" to indulge a child than to reinforce instruction and teaching with discipline. It's "easier" to do the dishes yourself than to remind your daughter it is her responsibility. "Easier" to get out the mower and cut the lawn than hassle your son into doing it. "Easier" to make the bed or pick up the dirty clothes than to see that your children do it. It is "easy" to let discipline slide because we haven't the mental and emotional energy to cope with it. *But we aren't doing anyone a favor when we do this!*

GUIDELINE THREE: *Administer discipline in private.* Discipline shouldn't be a family affair. It is very much a personal matter between a parent and his child. The purpose of discipline is to reinforce the teaching-learning process which develops a sense of right and wrong in the child. It is not to shame him, humiliate or anger him, which is exactly what happens when a child is disciplined publicly.

"And, fathers," wrote Paul to the Ephesians, "do not provoke your children to anger; but bring them up in the discipline and instruction of the Lord" (Ephesians 6:4, NASB).

Striking a child with your fist, slapping him, calling him names, pulling his ear or otherwise abusing him is *never* the proper way to administer discipline, and such forms of punishment only anger a child and create deep resentment in his heart as he grows older.

GUIDELINE FOUR: *Establish responsibility for the wrongdoing.* If you administer discipline in anger, your child may not be sure of the reason for which he is being punished. He only knows he did something wrong and "got it." A better way is to take the child aside and as calmly as possible talk with him until he realizes why his conduct was not acceptable.

How do you establish responsibility and show the cause-effect relationship of wrongdoing for which a child is being punished? It can best be done by asking a series of questions which cause a youngster to acknowledge wrongdoing. But be careful that you don't give him the opportunity to add a lie to the reason for which he is being punished.

Don't ask, "Did you take the money?" Rather ask, "Why did you take the money from my purse?" Pause to give him a chance to answer. Then continue, "You know that taking money which does not belong to you is wrong, don't you?"

Ask, "Do you understand that you were supposed to ask permission before you left our block?" Not: "Did you cross the street?"

Another good question is, "What did you do, Son?" The boy replies, "Well, *he* kept bugging me."

"What did *you* do?"

Finally he confesses, "I hit him in the face, but he was bugging me!"

GUIDELINE FIVE: *Show grief over the offense.* Saying, "This hurts me more than it does you" doesn't mean much to a child. He doesn't care that it hurts *you* inside. Rather, he cares that it is going to hurt *him* where he can feel it. Nonetheless, a wise parent makes his child realize that a parent *is* hurt in his heart when a child does wrong, just as our Heavenly Father is displeased when we are disobedient to His will.

A few moments of thoughtful silence allow a child time to think about what has happened and to sense the seriousness of what he has done. It isn't necessary for a parent to sit and moan every time a spanking is necessary—leave that to your child. But it *is* wise to demonstrate grief over the necessity of having to discipline him.

You need to emphasize the fact that when you discipline your child you are not rejecting him, but his act of disobedience. Because you love the child you care enough to take him aside, explain what is wrong and then to mete out discipline—but what kind of discipline, how much, and for how long?

GUIDELINE SIX: *Administer discipline firmly and thoroughly.* If a child has to be disciplined, do a good enough job of it so that he knows what is happening. When a parent whacks a child or slaps him across the mouth, he is not administering a thorough job of discipline. If discipline is necessary, spank hard enough and long enough to leave an impression, but not hard enough to bruise or break the skin. Proverbs 13:24 (NASB) says, "He who spares his rod hates his son, but he who loves him disciplines him diligently."

The Bible speaks of a "rod" as an instrument of correction (see Proverbs 29:15; II Samuel 7:14, Isaiah 11:4), and based upon the use of the Hebrew word, *shebet,* we can be reasonably certain that a rod was a stick for punishment. However, in some cases the rod was the staff of the shepherd (normally used to guide the flock). We do know that the rod or stick used for punishment was a neutral object.

Some child psychologists today do not advocate spanking with the hand because they feel that the hand which wipes away the tears and expresses love should not also be the instrument of discipline. If there *is* a detrimental effect in using a hand to administer discipline, what they are saying is consistent with what Scripture teaches. If you don't have a stick handy, then use a hairbrush, a ruler, a belt, or something that will injure pride but not leave permanent harm.

GUIDELINE SEVEN: *Allow a child to vent his emotions and then talk with him.* It is unfair to a child to give him a spanking and then say, "Don't you cry, or I'll spank you again!" If you've hurt his pride and his posterior as well, let him get it out of his system—at least to a reasonable extent. Don't shut him in a room. Rather, stay with him until he has stopped sobbing, then talk with him again to clarify why he was punished.

I would encourage you to put your arm around your youngster and pray with him, asking the Lord to help your child do the right thing and be obedient to Him. Encourage your child to pray with you, asking God's forgiveness and help in the future.

A word of warning: Don't ever use God as the "big stick" who is going to get a child for wrongdoing. Doing that can emotionally and spiritually hurt a child as he grows up thinking that God is out to get us. But do take advantage of the situation to explain that disobedience is sin, and that sin bears the consequences of punishment.

GUIDELINE EIGHT: *Once a matter has been dealt with, consider it forgiven.* Very clearly the Bible considers discipline as a teaching situation in that it likens the discipline of our Heavenly Father to the discipline of our earthly father and points out that love in both cases is the reason for caring (Hebrews 12:5-13).

When God forgives us, our sins are as far as the east is from the west (Psalms 103:12), and are forgotten (Isaiah 43:25). Accordingly, wrongdoing for which your child has been punished should be put away. Under no circumstances should other children in the family be allowed to tease or torment a child who has been disciplined.

GUIDELINE NINE: *Gear discipline to the age and offense of your child.* It is rather ludicrous to think that a mother should try to spank her sixteen-year-old son who is five inches taller than she. The Bible makes it clear that a child should be spanked when he is small. Proverbs 13:24, which speaks of the rod, says that he who loves his child disciplines him diligently—but the text literally reads, "Disciplines him early in the morning." Commentators agree that the writer is saying early in the morning of life when your child is still impressionable.

Discipline your children firmly, consistently, and lovingly when they are small and it will not be necessary to try to turn them over your knee when they are strong enough to turn *you* over theirs!

As a child grows older, restrictions can be just as devastating, if not more so, than physical punishment. When our son was hooked on electronics, about the age of twelve, the most effective punishment to him was to unplug his soldering iron and not let him work at his projects. With a teenager, restrictions may include limited use of the phone, or a restriction on activities or sports; but when it is meted out, stick by your decision no matter how loud the protest.

GUIDELINE TEN: *Balance discipline with personal attention.* Whenever it is necessary to administer discipline, a wise parent asks himself, *Why was this necessary?* Quite often the necessity for discipline is a red flag indicating a child needs personal attention, and he's going to get it even if he has to suffer for it.

There is a definite correlation between unacceptable behavior and the amount of time a parent spends with a child. With our three children, we have found that some time spent individually with them following the offense for which discipline was necessary does more to improve attitude than all the candy in the corner store. Nothing is a greater gift to your child, nor will anything contribute more to his good behavior, than the gift of yourself.

SOME THOUGHTS TO PARENTS, FROM A PARENT

Realize that discipline begins with YOUR life. Anna Mow says, "Most of the resentment against discipline is because parents are so undisciplined in their own lives." No parent can successfully discipline his child when he is undisciplined himself. Suppose you park yourself in front of the TV set and cannot pry yourself loose from it, yet try to teach your child the importance of diligently studying at school. We've got to learn to draw limits for ourselves as well as for our youngsters.

How about your emotions? Are they in check? Or do you allow yourself to fly off the handle and discipline your children in a rage? Let's face it—to suggest that a parent will never discipline his child in anger is absurd. (Bachelors and old maids spin such advice, right?) However, venting your anger on your child is quite another matter.

It is perfectly in order to express yourself by saying, "I get angry inside when you do that." Or, "I really hurt inside because you keep telling lies. We don't tolerate such behavior in our family." But letting your anger out through physical abuse or a torrent of abusive language is inexcusable and will do more harm than good.

How do you respond when God disciplines YOU? Are you rebellious inside because of circumstances you don't like? Is it also possible that your children's unacceptable behavior is merely a reflection of your own emotions? *Your* rebellion? You will find, if you haven't already, that our children mirror our own lives. Get uptight, and that tension is transferred to your children. They don't understand why, but they still get punished for it.

On the other hand, if you learn to relax in the promises of Scripture, being able to accept the fact that all things work together for good to those who love God (Romans 8:28), your kids will learn to unwind as well.

If you have lived your faith before your children, they will never forget it. Teenagers can chafe at your "straightlaced" restrictions, but they will never forget the love and concern that you showed them. Someday they'll come to the place where they can look back and thank God that you were the "meanest" parents in the world.

A word to dads. If you are serious about using the guidelines of Scripture as a guide in discipline, you must remember that the Bible consistently teaches that discipline is the responsibility of the father. I would encourage you to read through the Book of Proverbs and to mark every passage referring to fathers and discipline. Discipline is *your* responsibility.

Does that mean a wife should not discipline a child? No, but it does mean that when she must discipline a child it should be because you have delegated that authority to her. God still holds *you* responsible for reinforcing the teaching-learning process with discipline.

Generally, it should be dads who administer discipline; however, the impact of discipline is greatly diminished, if not completely lost, when a considerable period of time elapses between the time the problem arises and the time it is dealt with. It is much better for a mother to deal with the situation right then than to always say, "Your father is going to get you when he comes home tonight!"

But, Dad, if you fear God, don't abdicate your responsibility to discipline and let your wife be the sole administrator of corrections. Realize that God wants *you* to be a picture—imperfect as it may be—of His love and concern. You can't do it by letting the little lady handle all the problems of raising a family.

A closing word. Try to remember that God promises a reward when discipline is followed—the quiet growth of a child in God's grace and the development of his character. It's in Hebrews 12:11 (NASB): "All discipline for the moment seems not to be joyful, but sorrowful; yet to those who have been trained by it, afterwards it yields the peaceful fruit of righteousness."

It's all part of training up a child in the way he should go.

6

Conveying Values
to Your Children

6

When *Family Life Today* magazine polled parents from various strata of life to determine the areas of family living which they felt needed the greatest attention, the editors were surprised. Parents said that, apart from the importance of communication in family living, knowing how to teach Christian values to their children is the greatest single need of the Christian family.

Yet, parents who participated in the poll were uncertain as to what Christian values *are*. "Qualities that set you apart from the world," was one answer. "Conforming to the Scriptures," "A Biblical and godly system of ethics," and "A Biblical perspective on living" were other answers parents gave, according to the magazine's editors.[1]

Do you want to know how effective you are being as a parent in conveying your value system to your children? First, sit down together with your spouse and make a list of the moral and spiritual values which you want to convey to your children—a kind of heritage which you believe you are giving to them. Then—if you can stand it—sit down with your children (teens especially) and ask them to draw up a list of values which they consider to be important. Comparing the two may be quite a revelation.

We sometimes assume we are conveying our values to our offspring when actually we may be conveying a different set of values. But of one thing we may be sure: *Every parent conveys some sort of values to his kids.*

Consider the sad case of Robert Knowles. He thought he had the formula for raising children. He told the press that he had always believed a child would turn out just fine if the parents loved him, spent plenty of time with him, involved him in wholesome activities, and helped him get a balanced education.

Said Knowles, "Suddenly after seventeen years of dedicated effort, something happened to my foolproof plan. I found I was the father of a murderer." Knowles' seventeen-year-old son was sentenced to twenty-five years in prison after pleading guilty to the murder of a sixteen-year-old girl. Robert Knowles will be asking himself, *What went wrong?* for the rest of his life.

The bewildered father candidly confessed, "The shock, agony and soul-searching are unbelievable. Everything you believe in is gone in one bolt of lightning that rips your heart out at the same time. *What went wrong?* Nothing fits your notion of criminal behavior and what to do about it."

Many a Christian parent in shock has asked the same question. "What went wrong? Where did I fail?"

"One of my greatest heartaches," wrote a gray-haired father well in his 70's, "is that my children are not living for the Lord. They were all raised in a Christian home. In fact, my wife and I have spent most of our lives in the Lord's service, but more than anything else, we would like to see them come back to Him before we die."

Almost every week at least one heartbroken parent responds to my family living radio program and writes something like this: "Dear Dr. Sala: We were shocked to learn that our daughter is living with a man to whom she is not married. We did our best to raise her in a Christian home. She went to church and Sunday school with us, and what she is doing is contrary to the way she was raised. It hurts us deeply. We don't know what went wrong."

What went wrong? How do some parents succeed in sharing values with their children, while others see their kids grow up to reject almost everything of moral and spiritual value?

WHY DO SOME REJECT THE VALUES OF THEIR PARENTS?

I have served in various capacities as a pastor, counselor, and then for two years as a missionary—spending a large percentage of my time counseling with those involved in Christian ministries. As I worked with missionary children—some of whom became very bitter—I began to see "value systems" from a different light.

I don't consider myself a definitive voice in the matter, and I won't until my kids have grown up, married, and sired their offspring and they have adopted the same value system as their parents. But what I *have* discovered may help you keep from making some tragic mistakes.

Some parents begin too late in life to teach Christian values. I know that was true of one father whose wife called me and with tears in her voice said, "Bob has just been sentenced to a year in prison." The family had just started coming to church, and I had not really gotten to know them, but I did know that Bob's dad had recently found the Lord.

"Well, what happened?" I inquired.

"You see," began the mother, "Bob was driving home from the high school prom and he had had too much to drink. His car swerved into the chain-link fence dividing the freeway lanes, and the police charged him with drunk driving. He's been sentenced to prison for a year. Will you go see him?"

Of course I went to see him. There he was—a skinny, seventeen-year-old kid, locked behind bars with hardened criminals. He looked so forlorn and pitiful standing there in prison coveralls, his head shorn in prison fashion! I thought to myself, "What's a kid like this doing here?"

That afternoon I got acquainted with Bob, and, better yet, he got acquainted with Jesus Christ. Salty tears of repentance filled his eyes and brimmed over as he wiped them with the back of his hand. I was impressed with the sincerity he showed as he prayed to invite Jesus Christ into his heart.

Though I didn't tell Bob, I decided to go visit the judge who had sentenced him and tell him what had happened. The judge was impressed, but what he admitted impressed me even more. "I must have made a mistake," he said. "A year's sentence is much too severe for a first offense. Tell you what—I'll bring him back to court, lecture him, and put him on probation."

That he did! After a sermon that would have done justice to Billy Graham, the judge put him on probation. Bob and his fiancee, followed by his parents and me, walked down the aisle of the court and stepped in the foyer.

I noticed that Bob's dad was crying, and I reached over and put my arm around his shoulder. "It's okay, Dad," I said. "Everything will be all right now."

"It's all my fault," he sobbed. "Bob is simply following in my footsteps. Night after night he saw me come home drunk. God saved me, but he saved me too late to wipe out my example."

The good ending to that story is that the example of a father's conversion did speak to the heart of his son. I married Bob and his fiancee a while later, and they established a Christian home. But how much heartache and sorrow could have been saved had the parents only begun sooner to teach Christian principles to their son.

"DON'T DO AS I *DO*—DO AS I *SAY*..."

Another reason children reject their parents' Christian values is a separation in belief and practice. A less dignified synonym is "hypocrisy."

Behavioral scientists say that quite often there is a division between what people *say* they hold dear to their hearts and what they *really* hold dear. They may put up a good front with their neighbors and friends, but they can't fool their kids. Our lives speak louder than anything we can ever say!

At four o'clock one morning my phone rang. As I reached for the phone a mother sobbed, "We've just

learned that our boy, Dick, has committed suicide."
As in all tragedies there was a story behind the
story.

Dick went to church with his mother quite
faithfully as he grew up, but then in his senior year of
high school he went to work for two men who were
deacons in the church he attended. The two men
owned a shoe store, and Dick soon learned that their
"Christianity" didn't much interfere with their
scruples when it came to making a buck. During the
week they were dishonest and encouraged him to do
the same: "After all, business is business." Then on
Sundays they ushered and shook hands with people
and "played church," but Dick knew exactly what
was happening.

One Sunday morning he walked out of church with
his mother and slammed the door behind him.
"Mom, if that's Christianity, I don't want any part of
it. I'll never darken the door of a church again."

The next year Dick went on to the university and
began a long search for reality. For a while he
thought existentialism was the answer, but eventually Nietzsche and Kierkegaard left him still
wanting. He tried drugs, illicit sex, and travel. The
sad search ended in a cheap hotel room in Nome,
Alaska as he put a revolver to his temple and pulled
the trigger.

Who is responsible for what happened? Sure,
ultimately Dick will be accountable for his part in
rejecting the values of Christianity, but un-
questionably God will hold those two men responsible for their part in causing a boy to reject the values
of Christianity because he couldn't see beyond their
hypocrisy.

Kids reject values because parents assume they

have taught Christian values when they have really taught a system of "Christian" legalism. Merton Strommen heads the Merton Strommen's Youth Research Center in Minneapolis. Recently Strommen conducted an intriguing study involving 700 churches and well over 1,000 young people from evangelical churches. He directed a series of 200 questions to young people, then asked the parents the same questions, requesting that they indicate what they thought their children would answer.

He assumed that if parents and children answered in a similar fashion, it was an indication of a high degree of closeness and understanding. At the end of each survey, both parents and children were to complete a sentence. The teens were to finish, "My relationship to my parents is . . ." and the parents were to complete, "My relationship with my teenager is . . . ."

Some responses were shocking. One mother wrote, "My relationship with my teenager is a good one— we are close, and I feel she often confides in me and desires to please. We are pals." Her daughter wrote, "My mother is a witch, a snob, and a noisy Holy Roller."[2]

Philip Yancey, editor of *Campus Life* magazine and a man in touch with teens, asks the question, "Have we, in our insistence on rules and regimentation, missed the whole concept behind the family? It is a serious question, for our idea of a family must be firmly rooted in Scripture, and Scripture plainly denounces the type of law-oriented faith which Strommen uncovered. Could it be that teenagers are rejecting their parents' faith because it is a faith based on works and not on grace?"[3]

In some homes, the message children receive is

that Christianity is: not drinking, not dancing, not smoking, not indulging in premarital sex. Period. The list of taboos buries the reality that Christianity is really a dynamic relationship with a living, loving Saviour. Kids reject the values of their parents when they do not see the benefits of those values in their parents' lives.

The Jesus Movement of the 1960's was, in part, a reaction to the legalism of Orthodox Christianity. It wasn't Christ whom the kids rejected—it was the straw man, the rule-burdened caricature of Christianity, which their parents had projected. In the Jesus Movement, teens were presented with a living encounter with Jesus, and they bought it.

A MATTER OF PRIORITIES

Some reject the values of their parents because they are led to believe that the parents' work/ministry is more important than they are. Children resent the fact that parents don't have time for them. Then, when the parents *do* get around to spending some time with the kids, they are often so wiped out physically and emotionally that they have little to give.

No parent goes around verbalizing, "Look, kid, you are a hindrance to my work," yet that is exactly the message a youngster can get through attitudes as well as actions. Any dad who conveys the attitude, "Okay, Son, I gotta spend time with you to be a good dad, so hurry up and let's get it over with" might as well forget it. Kids are perceptive and know when you *feel* that way though you never say a word.

One Faith Academy student in Manila, Philippines, the son of a missionary, told me, "I actually believe my parents consider me a liability and a hindrance to their work."

That is exactly how one missionary's daughter felt, and she struck back hard. She was pretty and extremely talented—an accomplished musician. She came for counseling shortly after she had graduated from a Christian university.

Her eyes were red and swollen as she began to tell me that she feared she was pregnant by a young man she had been seeing. I wanted to cry out, "Why? Why did you do it when you have been raised so differently?" But I kept my mouth shut and let her talk. She eventually got it out.

The problem hadn't begun when she met the boy who had fathered her child. It had begun years before when her folks dropped her off at boarding school, and she felt a though she had been shoved out of their lives.

Over the years, those feelings of bitterness and resentment had built up and finally exploded. Her pregnancy was her way of fighting back. "I knew this would hurt them more than anything I could do," she said, not really caring that she was hurting herself even more.

One day Russ Lambert, principal of Faith Academy, and I were discussing values. I asked Russ to tell me, from his experience with the approximately 500 missionary kids at the academy, why he thought one "MK" will grow up accepting the values of his parents while another from very similar circumstances will reject them.

"It's the quality of time that parents spend with their children," Russ said. He went on to tell me of one father who travels a lot, often being away from home for long periods of time, but when the father is away, he writes to his children individually, and when he is at home, *he is completely at home.*

Whether it is your business, your ministry, or your involvement in church activities, you've got to remember that your family *is* your ministry and your first priority in life, and that your attitude when you are at home can make the difference in their accepting or rejecting your values.

Howard Hendricks tells of the time he was on a plane talking with a young business executive next to him. The moment he began to mention spiritual matters, the man bristled. "Would you mind if we changed the subject?" he curtly asked.

"Not at all," said Hendricks. "But I'd be interested in knowing why."

"I'll tell you why I'm not interested in Christianity," the man said. "Christianity robbed me of my parents and I'm not interested in anything that would do that." He told of a father who traveled extensively and a mother who was heavily engaged in Bible classes. "My parents were so busy leading everyone else to Christ, they lost their four boys, and there's not one of us who's interested. Now, would you mind if we change the subject?"[4]

Have you seen the "Charlie Brown" comic strip where Linus turns to Charlie and says, "My dad hates me." He explains, "Monday night he went to a PTA meeting. Tuesday night it was the School Board. Wednesday night it was the Board of Deacons, and last night it was bowling!" Next panel: "So this morning, he says to me, 'Hi, there!' And I said, "Who are you? I don't recognize you!'" Then Linus concludes, "He doesn't actually hate me . . . he just thinks I'm too sarcastic!"

Some children reject the values of their parents

*when they are not afforded the opportunity to de-
velop their own lives and personalities.* You may
have heard of "the minister's son syndrome,"—the
situation where the preacher's boy does everything
his dad says shouldn't be done. Why?

One of the reasons is that most leaders—whether
they stand in the pulpit or head a steel mill—have
dominant personalities. They have to be strong to
get where they are, but dominant personalities can
overshadow their kids who feel as though they aren't
given the privilege of being themselves.

Thrust into a mold they don't like, they end up
throwing the baby out with the bath water—rejecting
the values of their parents along with their parents'
life-style. At the same time, dominant personalities
often expect their kids to be "chips off the old block"
and, at times, the youngster just can't handle it. He
fails to measure up to his parents' expectations, which
results in self-criticism and low self-esteem. This
personal rejection of self may be characterized by the
child's adopting habits and values which he knows
will bring heartache to the parents.

THEY ARE "FREE AGENTS"

*Finally, children reject the values of their parents
because of their own rebellious, sinful natures.*
Ultimately, every person must accept responsibility
for his own decisions. Some parents punish
themselves by asking, "Where did we fail?" "How
could our kids have done this?" "Where did we go
wrong? . . ." when *they* didn't go wrong at all.
Their son or daughter, like the prodigal, stubbornly
refused to accept the values of his parents.

I know some gray-haired parents with grown

children who have adopted their values and are even involved in Christian work, while their other children, who grew up in the same godly home, rejected those values. We can't force a value system on our offspring, but we *can* do a lot to insure that they will grow up and want to adopt it.

HOW CAN WE CONVEY CHRISTIAN VALUES?

It's a challenging task God has given us. We've already dealt with several key principles such as teaching through our example, attitudes and words; communicating openly with our children; and disciplining them in firmness and love. These concepts form the foundation for seven essential guidelines which I believe parents *must* follow to succeed in conveying Christian values to their youngsters.

GUIDELINE ONE: *Get your priorities in order*. Parents often allow a false sense of priorities to envelop their thinking. They get the idea that youngsters are with them forever (and at times it does seem that way), so they reason there will be plenty of time to spend with their children . . . later on. When they finally start thinking about it, their kids are gone. The children have translated their parents' lack of time for them into personal rejection, and in retaliation, they have demonstrated their rebellion by tossing out values their parents hold dear.

They strike back by doing the very things they know will hurt their parents—so that finally they get the attention they have been denied.

Did the illegitimately pregnant girl I counseled not know that she was hurting herself and her future far more than she was hurting her parents who were 10,000 miles away? Certainly she knew, deep in her heart, but she didn't care. She only realized that this was the most brutal way she could strike back at them for denying her the time and attention she felt she deserved. It was a sad way of getting even for her feelings of rejection.

Parents, your first responsibility is not to your work, ministry, or other activities. It is to your family—to your spouse, and to your children. Yes, I know you believe that *mentally,* but *in practice* it may be another matter.

I know of one mother who was constantly being asked to assume responsibilities for various activities and functions because of her husband's position with an organization. Her husband's salary was set and paid by the board, so subtle pressures were put on her to "get with it."

As she put it, "They tell me that my home is my first responsibility, but when I won't take on more than I can handle because of my children, I know they resent it."

If you are a parent who is concerned about teaching your children Christian values, one of the first things you must really come to grips with is the truth that *duties do not conflict in the will of God.* Dad, God gave you the responsibility of a wife and a family before he gave you your present job or area of ministry, right? Then why set aside your responsibility to your family because of added responsibilities?

In his book, *Mamma Was a Missionary,* Charles Ludwig tells how he grew up in Africa as an "MK" whose parents ran a Girls' School. He tells how he was gradually pushed aside as the Girls' School grew. Resentment began to build.

> I seethed inside over these things, and one day I exploded. "All I hear is Girl's School, Girls' School, Girls' School," I shouted, losing complete control of myself. "When we pray, we pray for the Girls' School. When we get the mail, it is to see if there is a letter about the Girls' School. When we eat, the conversation is about the Girls' School. When we go to Misumu, we have to buy something for the Girls' School ... I tell you I'm getting fed up. I wish a bolt of lightning would come and smash the school."
>
> By this time I figured I'd earned a thrashing and that anything else I'd say would not merit extra punishment so I stood up and shouted, "I wish this mission, the Girls' School, and the hospital were all in ----!" I mentioned a place frequently referred to by theologians. "But instead of Mother reaching for a stick, she looked at me with a faraway look ... Then she said, "Charles, what would you like to have for Christmas?" This unexpected reaction stunned me for a moment. I could hardly believe my ears. When I regained my equilibrium, I replied, "I'll tell you what I really want, but I'm afraid you won't get it for me. I want a bottle of catsup!"[5]

Charles Ludwig didn't reject the values of his parents, but he did chafe under the collar because he felt that he was playing second fiddle to his parents'work.

How do parents avoid situations like this when they are busy and have a host of responsibilities?

Block out specific time each week for your family and your children. Realize that time spent with your family, whether it is fishing with your son or shopping with your daughter, is *not* wasted time. That leisure time may not be productive in terms of goods and services, but when it comes to your personal relationships, upon which a value system is built, you can't put a price tag on quality time with the children.

One mother began to realize her high school daughter would soon be leaving for college, and she felt as though she really didn't *know* her daughter. To remedy the situation while she still could, she told her daughter, "From now on until you go away to college, I'm taking each Monday evening and I'm going to spend it with you. We'll do anything you want—shop, sew, cook, walk together—anything."

The daughter, caught off guard, repeated, "That's silly, Mom—spending all that time together." But they started, and did all kinds of things. Some evenings they sewed; other evenings they went window-shopping. Some evenings they went to a little restaurant and had dinner and talked . . . and talked . . . and talked.

By the time fall rolled around, a new relationship had been forged between that mother and her daughter. When the girl went to college, she wrote long letters every week, and when she faced a crisis her first year away from home, she was close enough to her mom to turn to her for counsel and help.

GUIDELINE TWO: *Don't take values for granted.*

The title of this book implies that the training process of a child is a much more complex one than simply bringing a child into the world. If the values which have guided and molded your life are to be transmitted to the moral and spiritual fiber of your child, you must have a plan and work at it.

No great concert pianist would assume that his daughter is learning music theory because she grows up in his home. Neither are moral and spiritual values absorbed strictly from environment. Have a plan to *teach* spiritual truth as well as illustrate it with your life. That plan should include family worship, consistent participation in Sunday School and church, as well as a family forum for open, candid discussion. Some things are caught—other things are taught. They go hand in hand.

GUIDELINE THREE: *Live as consistently as you can.* Nobody is perfect, but most of us could do a better job if we really tried. A second-generation value system begins with you, and it is because of your life that a value system is transmitted to your offspring.

Of special interest to me has been second and third generation missionaries who have "been there," who know what it is to face hardships and loneliness, and to try to live on a pay scale that is substantially lower than that which could be earned at home. What causes these folks to go back? Invariably, the lives of the parents figure largely in the decision. Their children saw in their parents' lives the reality of their faith and a love for their work which was of far greater value than easement of the hardships.

Four renowned Bible scholars were at a conference together, and during one of the breaks the four got into spirited conversation about the relative merits of different translations. One said that his favorite was the *American Standard Translation* of 1901 because of its accuracy and faithfulness to the Greek and Hebrew.

Another disagreed. He felt that the *New English Bible* was much superior because of several poorly translated passages in the 1901 version.

The third held out for the revered *King James Version* which has been the standard of four generations.

The fourth man paused for a moment and then quietly said, "Personally, I prefer my father's translation."

"Oh," replied one of the men, "I didn't know your father had done a translation."

"Yes, most certainly. He translated the Word into his life."

GUIDELINE FOUR: *Confess your failures regarding your children.* When you have made a mistake, admit it! Don't pontificate as though you were perfect. On one occasion I felt that my son wasn't giving me the facts about a little altercation that had taken place with his sister, so I gave him a good spanking. Eventually, I found out that I had been wrong and he had gotten a spanking he didn't deserve.

Trying to practice what I believe is good for others, I bit the bullet and said, "Steve, I'm sorry. I spanked you when you didn't deserve it. I was wrong and I want you to forgive me for it."

"It's all right, Daddy," he said. "It just makes up for some of the ones I deserved and never got."

When you are wrong, admit it! You'll be setting a good example of honesty for your children to follow.

GUIDELINE FIVE: *Practice the primacy of unconditional love.* Your home should be a picture of the kingdom of God on earth—a kind of miniature church where the presence of Christ is felt. What God expects of us in relation to Him, He expects of us in relation to each other. Mainly, LOVE.

It was to parents that God said, in the Deuteronomy passage, "And you shall love the Lord your God with all your heart and with all your soul and with all your might. And these words, which I am commanding you today, shall be on your heart" (Deuteronomy 6:5,6, NASB). Then God instructed parents to teach these principles and precepts to their children. Their first responsibility was not to teach law, but to love God.

Both husbands and wives are to set love as a priority item (Ephesians 5:25, Titus 2:4, Colossians 3:14), and love is based on acceptance.

Unconditional love—the kind that is found in the kingdom of God—separates behavior problems from acceptance. ("If we confess our sins . . ." as recorded in I John 1:9, is found in the same Book with Ephesians 1:5: "He hath made us accepted in the beloved.")

What do you do when a son moves in with a girl to whom he is not married? Refuse to let him darken the door of your house? Curse the day you brought him into the world? Or, is it possible to separate acceptance of your son's actions from your personal acceptance of him as an individual? You *can* accept him and love him without accepting or condoning what he is doing.

Jesus did. The story of the woman taken in the act of adultery (John 8:1-11) makes that clear. Christ accepted her, and forgave her, but couldn't condone or accept her immorality. We can be the same example with His help.

GUIDELINE SIX: *Keep the channels of communication open.* Anger, frustration, constant preaching, sarcasm, and similar gestures are sure-fire ways to stop the flow of communication. Keeping communication lines open requires lots of genuine *listening* with an attempt to understand. If you can communicate with your child, you can help him see the consequences of his actions involving values and ethics. Where there is no communication, there is no possibility of influencing your son or daughter for good.

GUIDELINE SEVEN: *Garrison your offspring with a fence of prayer.* "Therefore I say unto you," said Jesus, "what things soever ye desire, when ye pray, believe that ye receive them, and ye shall have them" (Mark 11:24). Do you believe that? Do you also believe that God will honor your prayers and bring your son or daughter back to a place of faith as Proverbs 22:6 promises? Then pray more and criticize less.

No one delivering a eulogy over me will ever be able to give a "From gutter to God" discourse, because I was never there. In fact, I never even came close (less dramatic than the prison-to-pulpit scenario that sells books). But I can't take the credit for avoiding the "gutter."

I am convinced my mother's prayers kept me from wandering very far astray. When I was in high school and would come in late at night, often Mother would be on her knees praying. On many occasions I would get up in the morning, and Mother would be praying by the side of her bed or singing a hymn in the kitchen. I never asked, "Who are you praying for,

Mom?" Didn't have to. I knew!

Prayer is one of the best contributions to help insure that your son or daughter will grow up to adopt a Biblical value system.

What could be a greater heritage?

7

How to Tell
Your Children
About Sex

7

You might expect it in an underground newspaper or one of those magazines that cater to jaded, off-beat tastes, but it was in a legitimate city paper. The ad had been put there by a used-car dealer.

In letters one inch high, it really caught your attention if you were normal and under the age of seventy-five. The large print read, "SEX, S-E-X," and underneath were the words, "Now that we have your attention, let me tell you about..." and it went on to describe a used car for sale.

We use sex today to sell almost everything—from toothpaste to automobiles, from books to bologna. A large percentage of advertisements capitalize on sex to sell items that have not even the slightest suggestion of sex attached to them.

I think it is fair to say that never before has a generation been so bombarded with sex as we are today, and this is the result of two factors: The development of mass media—especially television and the movie industry which visually impress more people than at any previous time in history—and a sexual permissiveness in attitude which allows the mass media to be more explicit about sex than ever before. Instead of public decency being outraged, the public is inflamed with the desire for more.

Many parents are extremely hesitant to bring up the subject of sex or to answer the questions of a boy or girl, in spite of the sex-saturated environment in which a son or daughter is being raised. "There is far more openness in the discussion of sex today," we are told by newspapers and magazines, but I have come to the conclusion that much openness ends rather than begins at the front door of most homes.

Take, for instance, the discussion that took place as a family was riding through the country. As the car went by a stock feeding lot, a bull was mounted on the back of a cow. The seven-year-old pointed to the bull and said, "Look at those funny cows. What are they doing, Mommy?" There was an embarrassed silence, and very awkwardly, the little girl's mother replied, "Don't ask me now. Ask me at home sometime."

TEACHING OPPORTUNITY OR FIASCO?

A situation that could have easily been an excellent teaching opportunity turned into a fiasco. The little girl got the message that either she should not have asked the question, or the animals were doing something very wrong.

In most instances, the time a child asks a question is the best time to answer him—honestly and openly. But there is a very important principle which should temper *how much* you tell your child: *If he cares for details, he'll ask for details.*

By the time the child reaches age ten, a parent should sit down with him in loving conversation and be sure the child knows how babies are made and born, and that sex is a good but very private affair between a husband and wife. But in the earlier years, all of this may be too much for the child. For the seven-year-old girl in the above situation, it probably would be adequate to simply say, "that's how they make babies." Most children of that age (depending on their previous sex education) would be satisfied— and a deep technical discourse on insemination would only confuse them.

If, however, the child's curiosity is aroused and he asks further questions, answer these questions truthfully. For example, if the girl had proceeded to ask, "Why do they do *that* to make babies?" the mother or father could say something like: "The animal in back is the father, and the one on the bottom is the mother cow. That's the way she receives the seed from the father—it grows in her body and becomes a baby cow."

Give the child only what he asks for, but do so truthfully. After the first question-and-answer session, it should be stressed that "these are things we can discuss together, but not with others." Any private conversations between parent and child should be encouraged, but you will probably want to emphasize that when company is seated around the table is not a good time.

The birth of an animal—kittens, puppies, or whatever—is a wonderful teaching situation, especially when it is a pet which is loved by a child.

It might seem silly to some, but my wife prayed

when our expectant cat went into labor that our children might get home from school in time to see the kittens born. They did. Getting to see a live birth and understand the process as we explained what was happening did far more to complete their knowledge of how babies are born than a half dozen "talks" by school nurses.

When it comes to explaining the function of sex to their children, parents are often strangely silent. Yet, those same parents are often the ones who speak the loudest when it comes to condemning *their* parents for failing to give them sex instruction when they were young.

What parents do not understand is that sex education is taking place constantly in the world surrounding a youngster—on the theater and television screens, at the newspaper or magazine stands and certainly on the school playground. There may be no formal instruction in the classroom, but the educational process is going on all the time—in the jokes and half-truths the kids pass on to each other, by the stories they tell involving hearsay or the exploits of older brothers and sisters.

When the parent avoids the subject of sex, which is of normal interest to a child, he abandons the privilege of teaching his child. The parent who avoids the subject in all probability is leaving this area of his child's life open for instruction that often is perverted and full of misinformation coming from a variety of unqualified sources and teachers.

Dr. Lester Kirkendall, former professor of Family Living at Oregon State University, says:

> Most people assume that in the absence of direct instruction no sex education takes

place. Actually, the parents' reaction to themselves and to each other as sexual beings, their feelings toward the child's exploration of his own body, their attitude toward the establishment of toilet habits, their response to his questions and his attempts to learn about himself and his environment, their ability to give and express their love for each other and for him are among the many ways they profoundly influence the child's sexual conditioning....

The fact cannot be escaped. Parents cannot choose whether or not they will give sex education; they can choose only whether they will do something positive or negative about it, whether they will accept or deny their responsibility.[1]

Is there such a thing as a Christian concept of sex? If there is not, men and women have been deceived for centuries, for traditionally the sexual mores and ethics of believers have differed quite drastically from those of unbelievers. A Judeo-Christian sexual ethic grew out of sex instruction first given by Moses in the Pentateuch and amplified and upheld by the New Testament writers. Instruction regarding the place of sex in life and marriage was to be passed by the father to his son from generation to generation, as we have seen in Deuteronomy 6.

Instruction regarding the regulation and place of sex in our lives was given for two reasons. First, God wanted His people to avoid the sexual abominations which were practiced by the nations surrounding Israel. Second, He wanted them to know what His plan and purpose for their lives really was.

Today, centuries later, those two reasons are still valid. We must share a Christian concept of sex with our children because of the perversions and immoral practices which have become an accepted part of society today, and to give them positive instruction as to its God-given place in our lives.

If we fail to convey a Christian concept of sex to our children in our homes, where will they learn that God has endowed sex with sanctity? Where will they learn that God has graced sexual relations in marriage with virtue and tenderness? Where will they learn something of its regulation? If we parents fail, our kids will eventually grow up in a sex jungle with little, if any, positive guidance.

Many parents—whether from a lack of factual knowledge or a hesitance to talk about the subject— are not giving their children instruction about sex. These well-meaning parents want to believe that the silent witness of their lives overpowers the aggressive sexual openness of an immoral and perverted society today. Even today, counselors and pastors are still hearing the charge, "Mom and Dad never talked about sex when I grew up."

The home is a classroom where children must be taught what it means to be a father and a mother, and what the proper relationship of a husband is to his wife. Here kids learn sex is not dirty or something that takes place in the backseat of a parked car. The home must be the place where the male-female relationships are educational models which produce healthy, normal relationships in a future marriage and home.

"Yes, I know that I ought to give my children instruction at home when it comes to sex, but I just don't know where to begin." Those were the words of a young mother whose child had brought home a pornographic magazine.

GUIDELINES FOR SEX EDUCATION IN THE HOME

GUIDELINE ONE: *Provide a healthy setting for sex education by the environment in your home.* This first guideline deals with what you *are,* even more than with what you do or say. Since either negatively or positively, the home is a classroom, be sure that you have a proper understanding of this beautiful God-given relationship.

It is here that children learn that a mommy and a daddy love each other, because Daddy isn't ashamed to give Mommy a good hug and kiss—and Mommy returns the affection. The expression of love is not jaded or off-color; it is part of the emotional climate that teaches a child that we love and care about each other.

Occasionally, when I am counseling with a couple where one seems to be frigid or hesitant to express love, I will ask about the home in which he or she grew up. It is not unusual at all to hear someone say, "I never saw my father kiss my mother." Or "I never heard Dad tell my mother that he loved her."

That hesitancy to express love or affection, which may really be there, is a carry-over from what a child saw in his home as he was growing up. It is a false modesty, totally out of keeping with the Scripture or the world in which we live.

Believe it or not, there are hundreds of homes and marriages where a husband or wife never says, "I love you," and there is never any indication of love for a child to observe.

GUIDELINE TWO: *Help your child identify with his sexuality*. That's where the role of a father and mother must be straight in the thinking of parents. When there is no strong father, a boy tends to look to his mother for leadership. In many instances, this can have a damaging effect on the child.

Dominant mothers and insecure fathers who have little contact with their sons are planting the seeds of potential abnormalcy—particularly homosexuality. It's sound sex education to teach a boy to be a man and a girl a woman patterned after their own parents, who are secure in their own sexual identity. When our roles are confused, our kids will be confused as well.

GUIDELINE THREE: *Answer specific questions of small children as they arise, giving them clear, explicit answers to whatever is asked*. Generally, it is wise to give them enough to satisfy their curiosity, but not so much that they absolutely cannot understand it all.

A little boy came home from school with a questionnaire which was to be filled out and asked, "Mommy, what is sex?" Whereupon the mother said, "Son, sit down."

She then began to tell the boy the story of human reproduction in great detail. After the boy had listened with rapt attention for ten minutes, he said, "Mom, how can I get that on one line?"

The questionnaire asked for this information: "Name, grade, sex, and what subjects do you wish to take next year?"

When a child is small—under school age—his interest and attention spans are limited. Give him honest answers in simple terms. It is also best to answer questions as they come up. It really is not wise to say, "Wait until your father comes home from work and ask him then." By the time Dad has come home from work, the child has long since forgotten the question. Simple questions should be given simple, direct answers at the time they are asked.

To illustrate, here are two examples from Dr. Wilson Grant's excellent book, *From Parent to Child About Sex*. If a child asks, "Where was I before I was born?" *don't* tell him you found him under a lettuce leaf or that a friendly stork delivered him. Dr. Grant's suggested response:

> "You were inside of your mother. You began as a tiny egg smaller than a grain of sand. Over nine months you grew until you were the size of a baby. When you were big enough to live outside, you were born."

Or, if the child asks, "Are fathers necessary for babies to be made?" you might want to say something like,

> "Yes, mothers cannot make babies by themselves. When mothers and fathers get ready to have a baby, the father inserts his penis into the mother's vagina and deposits sperms that fertilize the egg in the mother's uterus. Then the egg begins to grow into a baby.[2]

As the child progresses in learning the basics of human conception, childbirth, and the related body parts, his questions will begin to broaden.

"Daddy, what's a rapist?" That question was asked by an eight-year-old girl who had heard that two women had been raped in her neighborhood, and because of that her parents had warned her against accepting a ride or talking with strange men who might stop her coming home from school.

The father could have said, "Ask your mother sometime." However, given the principle of answering a question when the child asks it, this would only give the impression that the parents' open invitation to questions is no longer valid.

The subject of rape is frightening enough for adults, let alone children, so the wise parent will answer truthfully but with tact. Again, a long list of the technical details is not necessary. If the child has had little previous sex education, the parent might reply, "A rapist is someone who does things which hurt a woman." For such a child, this response is probably an adequate initial response to satisfy curiosity, yet it enforces the fact that it's dangerous to talk or accept rides with strange men.

If the child has had some good talks with you, however, and knows the basics of the sex act and the sexual organs, you can be more specific. "A rapist is someone who forces a woman to have intercourse with him—sometimes by holding her down with a knife or gun. This hurts the woman because she doesn't want to have intercourse with him, and he's forcing her to do something against her will."

GUIDELINE FOUR: *Use the correct terminology when you are talking about human anatomy.* Howard Hendricks says, "If you are teaching a little child to make cookies, you do not say, 'Now we'll get those thingmajigs out of the drawer to measure baking powder and use that whatchamacallit there for flour.' You teach correct names because the child needs to learn. With a preschooler, you do not go into the technical jargon about the chemical changes in the baking of the cookie. You proceed on a simple and appropriate level. So it is with the facts of intimate life. We should name the parts of the body."[3]

Parents could avoid a great deal of misinformation by addressing themselves factually to kids' questions as they come up. Believe me, the education your child may receive on the school playground may be as bizarre as a space novel. Talk to him in direct, simple terms. This guideline is tied closely to another which cannot be separated from the proper use of terminology.

GUIDELINE FIVE: *Give a Biblical interpretation to sexuality.* Factual information must be put in the context of Scripture. Secular sex education deals with hard, cold facts of life apart from moral and spiritual significance. In many areas in recent years, school educators, sensing the problems and ignorance that exist, have attempted to put together programs of sex instruction. But those programs are usually lacking in moral and spiritual implications, so Christian parents object vociferously. No other aspect of human behavior is so intimately connected with a concept of moral right and wrong.

The great tragedy of our day is that so often sex is treated as a strictly physical relationship without moral or spiritual meaning. In your home, don't hesitate to talk about homosexuality, abortion, adultery, premarital sex, unmarried couples living together, and the multitude of sex-related subjects that are facing our children today.

Today, a new problem confronts our young adults—the epidemic of venereal disease that has literally swept the country. New strains of VD are being discovered that are so powerful antibiotics are almost worthless in combating them. Films seen at school produced by the Department of Health and Sanitation may tell your teens how to avoid it, but the deeper question, *Why avoid it?* is omitted. This should be part of our sex education in the home.

There is no avoiding the flood of sexuality in the world today. *Penthouse* and *Playboy* magazines both outsell *Time, Newsweek,* and *U.S. News.* Sex can't and shouldn't be avoided, but we will cry ourselves to sleep many nights if we fail to teach our children how to cope with this strong force and how to use it in its rightful God-intended place: the home, through marriage.

A survey of more than 1,000 teens sought to determine the part of their life in which they felt they were least prepared. Could you guess their answer? It was the area of sex. As our culture moves further and further from God-given norms, it is my belief that the Christian home has an even greater responsibility.

8

How to Succeed
with
Your Teenager

8

There are three categories of people who are interested in Scriptural guidelines for teens. First, the parents of a smaller child may anticipate probelms of the child's teen years and determine that God's Word, the Bible, will be a guide in the family. If we begin at birth and follow God's directions, we will eliminate 95 percent of the problems that often cause parents to age prematurely.

Second, a teenager, regardless of whether his parents are believers or agnostics, can determine that his life will be guided by the principles of Scripture. He can accept God's plan for his life. A thoughtful adult could direct his thinking to these guidelines.

There is a third category: those parents who have become Christians too late to have a Christian influence in the life of a son or daughter, or who have come to recognize the importance of following those Biblical guidelines too late to influence the children.

In those cases, it may take time. Right now your son or daughter may be firmly persuaded that God and those who believe in Him are left over from the days of Noah's Ark. Don't be upset by their doubts. Underneath their rebellion they will recognize changes in your life.

Let's begin with a great principle first laid down in the Ten Commandments. "Honour thy father and thy mother...," God said, "that thy days may be prolonged, and that it may go well with thee ..." (Deuteronomy 5:16). When the Apostle Paul quoted those words in his letter to the Ephesians, he prefaced them by saying, "Children, obey your parents in the Lord, for this is right" (Ephesians 6:1).

Two things need to be said at this point. The word "children" as it is used is not in reference to little children as we normally use the term. It includes that and more. The word that was used refers to young men and women as well. Like it or not, the Bible says that a young person's responsibility to be obedient doesn't stop until his own home is established, and then he is still to honor the father and mother who gave him his start in life.

The second thing that needs to be said is that this phrase "in the Lord" means the youth is to honor his parents in the spirit of doing it as if he were doing it for the Lord. It is the youth who obeys "in the Lord," not the parent who is "in the Lord." Young people who say, "I don't have to obey my parents because they are not believers" misunderstand what Paul is saying.

I like the attitude of a young hippie who was sitting on a curb when a policeman in street clothes came by and sat down beside him. After exchanging a few remarks, the cop said, "Say, what do they get for pot back where you come from?"

The hippie said, "You're not gonna believe this, but I just got saved and I don't use the stuff any more. I'm a Christian now."

The policeman said, "You're not going to believe this either, but I'm a Christian cop."

The youth responded, "Whadda ya know—a Christian cop! Well, put 'er there!" and the two shook hands.

Then the policeman asked, "Where you going to work?"

"Work?" responded the youth, "that's not for me." So the policeman told him how Paul said that if you don't work, you shouldn't eat, either. "Did you know that?" he asked as he pulled out a little New Testament, and shared Paul's words from II Thessalonians 3:10.

"Well," said the youth, "I didn't know it was there, but if it's in the Bible, then it's for me."

That's the right attitude for both a youth and parents toward Biblical authority.

UNDERSTANDING THE TEEN YEARS

In *Between Parent and Teenager,* Dr. Haim Ginott gives an incisive look at the turbulent years of a teenager:

> Many teenagers have an inner radar that detects what irritates their parents. If we value neatness our teenager will be sloppy, his room messy, his clothes repulsive, and his hair unkempt and long. If we insist on good manners, he will interrupt conversations, use profanity and belch in company. If we enjoy language that has grace and

nuance, he will speak slang.

If we treasure peace, he will quarrel with neighbors, tease their dogs, and bully their children. If we like good literature, he will fill our home with comic books. If we stress physical vigor, he will refuse to exercise. If we are concerned about health, he will wear summer clothes in freezing weather. If we are worried about air pollution and lung cancer, he will smoke like a chimney. If we prize good marks and academic standards, he will sink to the bottom of his class.

Bewildered, parents respond with a predictable sequence of desperate measures. First, we get tough. When this fails, we switch to kindness. When no results follow, we try reasoning. When gentle persuasion falls on deaf ears, we resort to ridicule and rebuke. Then we return to threats and punishment. This is the *modus operandi* of a mutual frustration society.[1]

Most parents would agree that a teenager is a strange contradiction of likes and dislikes, hate and love, fear and trust, peace and frustration, harmony and disruption. That's why these years have been described as a transition from the *organization* of childhood to the *disorganization* of youth, resulting in the *reorganization* of childhood.

The teen is not wholly to blame. At times he can't help feeling the way he does. His body is changing physically. Hormone changes encourage moodiness. At times the teen may dislike himself, along with brothers and sisters, parents, and everybody else who crosses his path.

Of course, everybody doesn't fall into the norm. There are those kids who don't happen to hate their parents, teachers, and life in general. But it happens frequently enough to make parents sigh in relief when the stage exhausts itself.

Part of the reason for the turbulence of adolescence is that two minds and sets of emotions are striving for the same body. The mind and emotions of the child/teen say, "I don't want to face the world of adults. I want to be mommy's little boy or girl who snuggles up close and gets tucked in at night." But, vying for the same space is the independence of the teen/child who says, "I want to do it myself. I don't need you anymore, and I don't want you kissing me goodnight or telling me what to do." Ambivalence is generally a characteristic of teenagers.

This ambivalence contributes to the dilemma of parents. How do they help when help is resented? How can they provide security and stability at the same time they are gradually teaching a youth to exert independence? How can they communicate when communication is considered an intrusion into the private world (if such a thing exists) of a teenager?

GUIDELINES FOR BETTER PARENT-TEEN RELATIONS

Many parents become frustrated when a child reaches the teen years. They seem to eagerly await the day Son or Daughter finally marries or moves out—anything to eliminate friction in the home. Are the teen years something merely to be endured, or can they really be enjoyed? The answer depends on the actors in the drama that takes place in the home, and to a great extent, on what has happened before a child becomes a teenager.

GUIDELINE ONE: *Remember that your son or daughter is facing a transitional period.* Think back to when you were a teenager. Weren't you in the process of "finding yourself," too? Isn't that why you pulled some of the crazy stunts you did?

A teenager is in the process of becoming. He's beginning to answer the questions: *What do I want to do with my life? What kind of person do I want to be?*

The most important thing in the world to a teenager is not the world's economy, the Middle East crisis, the stock market, or even pollution and ecology. Peer acceptance—*What do my friends think of me?*—is the most important single factor to a young person.

Radio and television don't exactly calm the troubled waters of adolescence, either. They make him aware of the lastest fashion and hairstyle. They tell him how to sweeten his breath, lose his dandruff, whiten his teeth, be a success with the opposite sex, and on and on. To such media bombardment, add the natural awkwardness of a teenager and you have a formula for very real frustration. But, a ray of hope: The teen isn't going to be this way for the rest of his life. If a parent can remember that these years will "come to pass," it helps keep perspective.

GUIDELINE TWO: *Be a parent—not a teen.* A lot of misguided mothers think they have to dress, act and talk like a teen to understand a teen—which is a lot of nonsense. First of all, most mothers don't have the figure to wear something that would have looked good on them twenty years before. They are a generation apart and no amount of mascara or long stringy hair will make them a teenager again. Love, acceptance and understanding will do more to open the doors of communication than trying to talk, look, and act like a teen. A healthy relationship is based on respect for what you *are*—not for what you wear or say.

GUIDELINE FOUR: *Keep the channels of communication open.* A study of several hundred teenagers between the ages of fourteen and eighteen indicated that most teens who lose touch with their parents do it between twelve and thirteen years of age. Yet, 40 percent of those who participated in the survey felt that they still had good communication with their parents.

Generally, when teens have problems talking to their parents, it is the result of a strained relationship that grows more and more tenuous as time goes on. Usually, it isn't difficult to foresee a problem in communication developing, but many parents fail to do anything to correct the situation until it is too late to avoid it.

GUIDELINE FIVE: *Parents should differentiate between acceptance and approval.* There are times when very clearly a parent cannot approve of what a teen does—especially during the late teen years when a child is no longer under the direct authority of the home. Often, in the thinking of a youth, unacceptable behavior is translated as rejection. There may be times when you don't approve of what your teenager does, yet you love him and can still be one of the greatest forces for good in his life.

I'm thinking of the mother who boasted, "When my daughter got pregnant, I threw her out of our home. I'm not going to have a daughter like that living under my roof." What happened? The girl simply moved into her boyfriend's apartment, while the mother's righteous wrath grew cold and hollow.

Or what of the father who says, "If my son won't work, he's not going to stay at home and sleep until noon." So out the door the son goes and moves in with a group who have no thought for morality or decency.

A parent can differentiate between acceptance and approval by making it crystal clear that—while he will not approve of his son's or daughter's wayward actions, he will still love and accept him as a person.

GUIDELINE SIX: *Go easy with your criticism.* This is a hard one. "You'll never amount to anything," "I'm wasting my breath on you," and "Is this what I get for everything I've done for you?" are examples of timeworn cliches which usually fall on deaf ears. Criticism of a teen usually brings about estrangement and separation. Lectures and condemnation, especially in front of friends, aren't worth the emotional energy it takes to deliver them.

There is a better way! First, calm down so that you are fully in control of the situation, then sit down and have a straight talk with your offspring. Parents ought to be parents. They are not school counselors, friends or even just good buddies. They are responsible and have to express their concern and guidance in the best way possible. That can't be done when a parent is angry.

You may be tempted to set aside your better judgment when a son or daughter says, "Why can't I? Everybody else gets to." You may be the meanest parent in the neighborhood—mean enough to protect your son or daughter from some of the forces that would destroy his life, mean enough to keep him sane and sober in school instead of in the psychiatric ward of a hospital trying to fit his mind back together as the result of drugs. Criticism doesn't help much, but constructive guidance can save the life of your son or daughter.

GUIDELINE SEVEN: *Surround your son or daughter with a fence of prayer, asking God to guide and direct him.* Remember the words of Scripture, "Train up a child in the way he should go: and when he is old, he will not depart from it" (Proverbs 22:6). I have no ironclad guarantees that your son or daughter will not do things you don't approve of, but I *can* guarantee that if you raise him by the principles outlined in Scripture, he'll eventually *return* to the path that you've walked, thanking God for a mom and dad who cared enough to guide him to maturity.

GUIDELINES FOR PARENTS OF YOUNG ADULTS

Psychologist Henry Brandt says, "Your children will need your guidance the most between ages sixteen and twenty." Yet these years are often the most difficult in terms of teens accepting advice from parents. During the late teen years, three critical decisions are usually made: (1) the decision to go to college or to work; (2) the decision regarding an occupation; and (3) the decision regarding a marriage partner.

At times a parent may feel torn—should he let a son or daughter fail and make mistakes which will hurt, or should he guide him around some of the hazards that could really hurt his life and future? That, of course, is part of the parental challenge that requires sober, delicate handling.

For years the thoughtful parent has tried to groom a son or daughter for independence. In spite of the fact that some parents refuse to acknowledge it, a parent knows that a son or daughter isn't a permanent possession. A child comes into the home as the loan of a life.

From the first day, that child's training leans toward the goal of mature, sober judgment. But when the child is mature, and the parent must relinquish control, it is often difficult. It is hard for a mother to really "cut the apron strings" and not continue to think of her eighteen-year-old as her little boy who has to be told to wipe his feet at the door and wear his rubbers in the rain.

I'd like to share some guidelines to help parents across the troubled waters of young adulthood.

GUIDELINE ONE: *Let your child be himself.* If you will think back over a few years, you probably did some things *you* thought were cute—but your mom and dad might not have thought they were so funny. Sometimes our clothes and styles fall into this category. As parents, we live in a certain world and we are quite sure that we want our teens to fit the same mold—forgetting that our mold is dated.

As much as possible, let your children make their own choices. I think the words of Paul can be applied to family living when he said, "If it be possible, as much as lieth in you, live peaceably with all men" (Romans 12:18).

A generation ago, T-shirts and levis (usually pretty dirty) were the standard equipment for boys, and girls added bobby socks. Today the levis or blue jeans are just more fashionably faded and frayed, and kids have taken off their shoes. That doesn't mean that there isn't a time to dress neatly, but if you can stand to let them "do their own thing" as much as possible, it's a good start.

GUIDELINE TWO: *Don't impose your own unfulfilled ambitions on the future of your son or daughter.* You wanted to become a doctor, yet because of the economy you couldn't make it, and ended up in a sales position. From the time your little boy started school, you kept pounding into his thinking, "You're going to be a doctor someday."

But now your son is in college, and he's failed chemistry for the second time. He barely made it through biology, and he's not sure that he could name more than a dozen of the two hundred-plus bones in the human body. What's the prospect for your son becoming a doctor? Pretty poor.

So what do you do—rant and rave, and try to shame the child into becoming what *you* want him to be? Or realize that perhaps his greatest happiness in life might be in business instead of medicine? As parents we must learn to accept the uniqueness of our children's aptitudes and interests and let them make their own decisions about the future.

GUIDELINE THREE: *Don't use criticism to guide the thinking of a son or daughter.* High school and college-age kids—just like youngsters—test us to see our reactions. They can come up with some real shockers, but they come on with a positive "This is where it's at" approach. Like the son who announced at breakfast, "I think we ought to bomb all the refineries in the Arab countries. That's the way to put an end to the oil crisis."

His dad responded, "That's stupid. Where'd you learn that—from that dumb radical teacher at school?" What happened? The son grew irritated and withdrew. The next time he will hesitate to express himself at all.

Questions that will help a child think through the implications of an act are much more constructive. In the above situation, the father might have said something like this: "Let's think it through as if it actually happened ... what would the Arabs do next if we were to bomb their refineries? How about the Russians? What would be our response? Would this procedure actually help or hurt in the long run?"

Kids live for the "now" and often don't think about the implications of some remarks and decisions. You, as a thoughtful parent, can help them see beyond the "now" to the serious implications of life's decisions ten and twenty years from now.

GUIDELINE SEVEN: *Sift the trivial from the important.* If you saw a four-year-old playing with a butcher knife, you would take it away; yet I have known parents who refused to acknowledge the signs that a teenage son or daughter was playing with potential dynamite until it had exploded and tremendous damage was done. The dynamite could have been labeled sex, drugs, or any number of things.

"But, don't all teens have to experiment for themselves?" some parents may ask. If you mean, "Don't all young people have the right to determine how much it takes to do permanent damage to their bodies or brains," you are asking a serious question.

On many occasions I have counseled with parents who said, "We saw these things happening, and just couldn't believe that it was true. We looked the other way until it was too late to do anything about it."

One wise father sat down with his son and said, "Son, we know you're on drugs. We tried to believe that it wasn't true, but we can't any more. We're going to stand by you and see you through this. We're going to help you rejoin the human race." It was a long, slow road back, but the son entered a hospital, and made it with the help of his parents.

A word of caution: You shouldn't expect your son or daughter to measure up to a standard when you don't measure up yourself. Parents who drink or smoke have a hard time convincing their children they shouldn't try alcohol, tobacco or drugs. A young woman wrote:

> I'm a 19-year-old girl who is getting more and more confused about the world's morality. Who decides what is morally right? My parents? Society? The law? Or should I make the decisions myself? My parents are divorced and I live with my mother. She keeps company with a nice enough man, but they go away together for weekends, and I'm sure they do more than hold hands. I don't know why they don't get married.
>
> Meanwhile, my mother doesn't want me to stay out too late with my boyfriend. He's in law school and we can't afford to get married until he graduates .... I'm sure my mom thinks it's okay for her to do what she does, but she'd have a fit if I did it. How come the difference in standards?

This parent has ceased to have any leverage in guiding the future of her child. When you, as an adult say, "Do as I say—not as I do," you might as well not waste your time. Your son or daughter will do whatever happens to please him, and you as a parent won't be very convincing in your protest.

GUIDELINE EIGHT: *Once your child has joined his life's partner in marriage, help him to "leave" you.* God in His wisdom foresaw the all-too-common "in-law situation" and presented to Adam and Eve, the world's first parents, a preventative. "Therefore shall a man leave his father and his mother," God said, "and shall cleave unto his wife: and they shall be one flesh" (Genesis 2:24).

The "leaving father and mother" is a command to the new husband to leave his parents *physically* and *emotionally* for the sake of a healthy marriage relationship with his new partner. But it also means that the mother and father must *allow* him to leave. Failure to cut the apron strings will only make Mom and Dad a source of emotional tension upon the child's new relationship with his spouse.

Some wise parents I know counseled their daughter, "Once you have married, don't come running back to Mother. You've got to learn to live together." They were saying that, much as they loved their daughter, her home would now be with her husband. Mom and Dad's place would no longer be a shelter to run to when the inevitable arguments sprouted in the new marriage.

Finally, a word of comfort. There comes a time when a parent has done his best, when he must put the life of his child in God's hands, claiming the promise of Scripture: "Train up a child in the way he should go: and when he is old, he will not depart from it" (Proverbs 22:6).

The Bible is replete with examples of men like Jacob, who spent years wandering far from home and then finally returned to the faith of their fathers. The way of the prodigal is hard and filled with thorns, but God has a way of bringing a person back to a place of faith and trust.

At times I have had to tell parents that they have done everything they can do. Now they would have to put their son or daughter in God's hands and let Him do His work in that life. Many times a rebellious youth has to go to the end of his rope to find God. "Trust in the Lord with all your heart," wrote Solomon, "and do not lean on your own understanding. In all your ways acknowledge him, and He will make your paths straight" (Proverbs 3:5,6, NASB).

9

Making
Family Worship
Come Alive

9

Dr. Howard Hendricks relates the story of the great British pulpiteer, Richard Baxter, who accepted the pastorate of a prestigious church filled with wealthy, influential and sophisticated members. For three years, this godly man poured out his soul, preaching his best with all the passion of his heart. But his best efforts met with little success.

"Finally," says Hendricks, Baxter "threw himself across the floor in his study and cried out, 'O God, You must do something with these people or I'll die!'"

And what happened? Baxter said, "It was as if God spoke to me audibly, 'Baxter, you are working in the wrong place. You're expecting revival to come through the church. Try the home!'"[1]

Richard Baxter began visiting the homes of his people, and everywhere he went, he helped families organize times of family worship so that they could touch God together. The Spirit of God began to change hearts and lives, and in the months and years that followed, that congregation was fired with the power of God.

Touch the home, fire it with the presence of God, and churches and nations will be different.

WORSHIP AS A FAMILY—WHOSE JOB?

The church alone can't instill moral and spiritual truth in the hearts of our children. Compare the amount of time your son or daughter spends in church and/or Sunday school with the hours of secular education or the number of hours in front of the television set. There's just no way even the best church leaders can counter the secular influence of today's world in the amount of time they have to work with a child.

If you think going to church for an hour on Sunday is enough for God, you've just divided life into the *secular* and the *sacred.* You've put a tag on going to church and reading a Bible—sacred activities— versus the rest of the week—secular activities. By going to church for an hour on Sunday you are, in effect, saying, "God, I've taken care of You; now leave me alone so I can enjoy the rest of the week."

You've missed the whole thrust of what Christ came to do—to take faith out of the temple and put it in the hearts of men. He's not a God whom we meet for an hour on Sunday—just to be on the good side of the angels. Rather, Christ is a living Person who wants to be part of everything we say and do—seven days a week, twenty-four hours a day.

As a parent, just how do you plan to instill Christian character and fiber in your children? Do you have any spiritual goals for them?

Chances are you have a plan for your children's education. You have a pretty good idea where you want them to go to school and what you would like to see them do with their lives. But in the process of gaining an education, your child can become an intellectual who is morally and spiritually bankrupt—capable of earning a living, but never learning how to live. Is that what you would want to happen to your son or daughter? Of course not!

If you are serious about nurturing the spiritual life of your children, you must have some plan when it comes to sharing the truth of God's Word.

Who's going to initiate this plan and keep it going once you have begun? Many men say, "Let my wife do it—she's better at talking than I am!" The husband who does this not only fails in his responsibility to his family, but he also misses one of the greatest joys of life—leading his family in spiritual truth.

The Bible puts the responsibility of leadership on the shoulders of the husband or father when it instructs, "For the husband is the head of the wife, even as Christ is the head of the church . . ." (Ephesians 5:23). That headship means responsibility for their physical welfare and their spiritual welfare as well.

Often I am visiting a home at mealtime. When we sit down to the table, the kids grab their forks, ready to spear the first hand that reaches for the platter before they can grab it. Just then the wife will sheepishly say, "Reverend, would you lead us in prayer?" Or the husband will nervously say something like, "Well, since you're here, why don't you say a prayer for us?" By his manner, that father

143

is telling me that when grace is said at a meal (which isn't very often), it is his wife who says it.

Dad, it's time to assume your responsibility and realize that if you don't lead the way, your wife may have to—not because she wants to, but because you're too much of a coward to be the spiritual leader of your own family.

IS IT REALLY WORTH THE BOTHER?

Dr. Pitirim Sorokin, former chairman of the Department of Sociology at Harvard University, sees a definite relationship between family devotions and a successful home and family life. This distinguished sociologist has observed that where "the family practice of Bible study and prayer is daily observed, there is only one divorce in every 1,015 marriages."[2]

What happens in your home will undoubtedly guide the spiritual destiny of your children's future, whether it is for good or bad. Dr. Henrietta Mears, for many years one of the foremost world authorities on Christian education, said that a college student doesn't go to college and lose his faith. She contended that he didn't have any faith to begin with. The assault on the faith of a student in the college years often results in the spiritual shipwreck so prevalent today; however, the parent who has wisely instilled spiritual concepts in his children through family worship is building a spiritual bridge across the troubled waters of college years and young adulthood.

Take Chuck Farah, for instance. Chuck was raised in a Christian home where he was taught the Word of God. As a youth, he memorized Scripture which remained in his subconscious, regardless of how it was challenged by atheistic teaching. During his graduate studies, Chuck began to doubt some of the truths he had learned at his mother's knee and, for a period of time, waxed in the despair of atheism. Walking the streets of Edinburgh, wrestling with the question of faith in God, he began to recall the Scriptures he had learned as a child. It was the Word of God he had learned in his home that brought him back to a place of faith and trust.

It has been during our times of daily devotions that two of our three children have asked to pray to invite Jesus to become their personal Saviour. Is it worth the time and effort to make some preparation? You can be sure it is!

Okay . . . perhaps you recognize that you *need* to have family devotions—a time each day when you stop to communicate with God and discuss spiritual applications as a family. You know you ought to, but when is the best time?

"Well, anytime!" you might say. No—not really, for "anytime" is usually "some other time," and some other time never quite comes around. You've got to decide, "We are going to have daily family devotions in our home," and then cling to that resolve with the tenacity it takes to collect a loan from your brother-in-law.

If you are to succeed in a program of family devotions, you will have to consider family schedules and then decide upon a definite, fixed time when you can usually be together. You'll need a minimum of at least five minutes, and I suggest that you take at least ten. Ten minutes out of a twenty-four hour period won't seriously cramp your schedule, but it can make a tremendous difference in what happens the other twenty-three hours and fifty minutes.

The time of day you meet together is completely dependent on your schedule. If you can do it, I suggest taking time immediately after breakfast, because you then have the rest of the day before you. But if morning isn't best for your family, then decide when you can all be together—perhaps immediately after dinner or early in the evening. The important thing is that you set a regular time and then try to stay with it.

HOW *NOT* TO HAVE FAMILY WORSHIP

Before I share with you a plan that will succeed, let me give you a little insight into what NOT to do, based on the mistakes and failures of thousands of people. The following are ways that you can kill a program of family devotions before you really get it off the ground—*and these are 100 percent guaranteed!*

Give up as soon as you've missed devotions a few days! "We started having family devotions, but it just didn't last!" is a lament that I have heard over and over again. It worked great for a few days, then you got busy and gave up.

Great! the devil laughs up his sleeve, *got you right off the bat.* Your alarm clock went off too late and you were rushed. The phone rang just as you were ready to begin. The toast burned—anything to diminish your time and increase your irritation, so you wouldn't feel like picking up the Bible. Someone wisely said, "The chains of habit are too small to be felt until they are too strong to be broken."

If you miss devotions for a day or two, it is hard to begin again. You have to be sold on the importance of what you are doing!

Do the same thing every time! This is guaranteed to bore everybody to tears in twenty-one days or less. (You might even want to have your favorite meal for supper every night, too—after all, if something is good, why settle for less?) On the serious side—there is a rich variety in the Bible. It is an anthology of history, poetry, prophecy, narrative, and spiritual guidance. If you do the same thing every time in your devotions, it will lack the freshness and variety which makes this time stimulating and refreshing.

Turn your family devotions into a discipline session as often as possible! As soon as you have read the Bible, turn to your son and gravely demand, "What is this report your mother has given to me about your getting into trouble at school today?" Or, "I want to know why you and your sister had an argument over who cleans up your rooms." This way your kids will dread family devotions and begin to think of the Bible as a kind of "book of the law" which Dad reads just before he chews them out.

A really intelligent, discerning child may be able to sift out the spiritual impact of family devotions from the discipline, but it is unwise to confuse the two in the minds of children.

Under no circumstances should you allow the rest of the family to participate! Parents, do it all! When a family begins to have family devotions and I ask the father, "How's it going?" The response is usually quite positive: "Fine! It's been a real blessing to us." But occasionally I will ask, "How is it going?" and the response is, "Well, to be perfectly honest, pretty bad."

"What are you doing?"

"I read the Bible every night and then I pray."

"What does your wife do?"

"She doesn't do anything, 'cept tell the kids to shut up while I read."

"What do your kids do?"

"Nothing, 'cept squirm and wait for me to get done."

That's the problem right there—one person doing it all without allowing the entire family to participate.

Get out of fellowship with the Lord! That will stop the best program of family devotions for sure. After all, who feels like talking to the Lord when some things have come between you and Him? Get a little angry with God, and you sure don't feel like opening His Word.

Get in a good argument with someone in your family and you'll feel the same way. You'll be convinced family devotions aren't for you!

Before I discourage you any further, let me share with you some guidelines that will work in making this time a real blessing to your family.

GUIDELINES THAT WORK

GUIDELINE ONE: *Have a plan.* The general organization of this time together has a lot to do with the success or failure of what you do.

There are three ingredients which go into a successful family worship program:

    1. God's Word, the Bible, which is our guide and strength in life

    2. Prayer, which is conversation with God

    3. Memorization of Scripture geared to the needs of your family

The best method for your family depends on the age of your children and what you wish to accomplish. If you have small children, begin with the great Old Testament stories and the narrative portions of the life of Christ which are story-like in nature. A little four-year-old doesn't have much interest in the four horsemen of the Apocalypse or the Book of Revelation, because he doesn't understand them. Yet a fourteen-year-old may have a great interest in prophecy.

As children grow older, they are able to grasp the great principles of the Epistles and the Book of Acts, the deeper truths of God's Word.

GUIDELINE TWO: *Be definite, yet flexible, in your plans.* A great general is quoted as saying that what really counts in battle is not the ability to attack but the ability to follow through with a sustained offensive once the attack has begun.

When you have made the decision to begin a program such as I'm outlining, you will find that for the first few days, maybe weeks, it will go quite well. Then you will get busy and miss a day or two. About that time you wonder whether family devotions will work for you. Believe me, it will—provided you stay with your plan.

When you have chosen the best time for your family to be together, make that time a habit. But what happens when it is impossible to meet at the time chosen? Have your devotions at a different time of that day. Be definite ("We *will* have devotions today . . ."), yet flexible (". . . even if we have to change the time."). Sometimes our schedules just don't happen to fall into neat little patterns and we are tempted to quit. When you feel like that, be persistent.

GUIDELINE THREE: *Variety is a must in presenting the Word.* If you start with Genesis, don't try to read right through the Bible. You may want to read through the book of Joshua and talk about the conquest of the Promised Land. Then read the book of Ephesians, then the Gospel of Mark, then perhaps the Psalms or the Book of Acts.

At times in our family, we have passed out paper and had everyone tuck a sheet in the flyleaf of his Bible. Then we would ask one to make a list of the miracles, another to make a list of what Jesus said about forgiveness, or what He said about love. This not only provides variety, but also involves each person as an active participant.

Some times we have one child read from one translation and a second and third read the same passage from a different translation, comparing what they say. We try to use variety in every aspect of what we do—yet stay with the three solid ingredients:

1. The study of the Word
2. A time of prayer
3. Memorization of key verses and passages geared to the needs of our family

Variety in your prayer time is also necessary. After the Scripture is read, we chat together for a few minutes, and the one leading the devotions usually asks, "Well, what shall we thank the Lord for, and what do we want to pray about?" Everybody shares. Then we pray. Sometimes one will lead, then another. At times, we pray around the table, but at other times we will pray in conversational prayer with each joining in short sentence prayers as he wishes to.

We have a standing rule in our family and I suggest it for yours. *Nobody laughs or pokes fun at what the other says or does when it comes to our expressions of prayer during family worship.* This especially applies to older children who might be tempted to snicker or laugh at what a smaller child prays about. We've tried to teach our children that we who are older must help younger brothers and sisters to grow, and if we laugh at what is serious to them, they will not want to share the next time.

This means your three-year-old may pray for his doggy or his cat, or talk to the Lord about butterflies or caterpillars. Let him. They are important to him.

What about family devotions away from home? On vacations, many families give up on family devotions. But that's like saying, "God, we are going to be away for a couple of weeks. See You when we get home!" Actually, those leisure days can be some of the greatest times of your life for devotions.

Our children will never forget some of the times that we have been away from home and stopped somewhere for ten or fifteen minutes to share the Word. On one occasion, we were traveling through Smoky Mountain National Park and stopped where a lookout enabled us to see the vast valley and opened the Word. It was during the fall when the leaves were brilliant shades of red, orange, and gold. We read the first three chapters of Genesis and talked about God's creative power as we viewed that panorama of beauty.

Our children still talk about the time we were in Europe and joined hands in prayer in the shadows of the beautiful Alps. Those times of family worship away from home help demonstrate to the children that we want to serve God on vacation as well as at home.

GUIDELINE FOUR: *Include your entire family in devotions.* Whatever secrets we have discovered in our own home, we have found that one of the most important is to bring our children into this time together as equals and fellow participants—not as kids who are going to get an injection of Bible as a kind of spiritual vitamin B. This is why the attitude of parents is so important.

Those who have been guests in our home will tell you that this is a time when our children look forward to opening the Word together. It is a family time when we not only teach spiritual truths to our children, but join hands and hearts as a family, looking to God for our needs and those of the rest of the world.

How do you involve all the members of a family—especially when they may range from small children to teens? First, get comfortable. Who says that you have to sit in a straight-backed chair to read the Word or pray? You may stretch out in the living room, sit on a woolly rug, pull your chairs together in a circle on the patio, or just remain at the dinner table and relax together.

The father is the one who should guide the time, but he should involve all the family. At times I have said, "Okay, this week each of you children will have the responsibility of planning family devotions." Does it work? You bet it does.

If you are studying a book of the Bible, let each know which chapter or portion he is to cover, but how it is done is up to the individual. You may be surprised at what your children come up with.

We have listened to Ethel Barrett stories (a Christian storyteller who has a number of children's records which our children have enjoyed), and at other times we have read passages in unison, sung hymns, listened to a gospel recording, or acted out favorite stories such as David and Goliath, or Jonah and the great fish.

When our children were small, either my wife or I would talk with the one responsible for devotions before the meal to see what was planned, but we let him lead—selecting what was to be done and how we were going to pray together.

This, of course, assumes that your children have observed *you*, so they have an idea of what can be done. If this is your first attempt to have devotions, wait for a few weeks to try this, so your children can first learn from you. But when they understand what family worship is about, you can trust them to come up with something original and worthwhile almost every time.

When our children were smaller, we would clarify Scripture with paraphrases such as Ken Taylor's *Living Bible* (which he wrote so that his ten children could grasp the Bible in simple, relevant terms). We have also found his *Living Stories for Children* to be especially helpful. In this devotional book for children ages five to twelve are passages of Scripture, followed by a number of questions which can be used to guide discussion.

What about devotional guides? Several organizations publish very fine daily devotional guides which can be purchased in Christian bookstores. These daily guides have been a great blessing to thousands, but they must never become a substitute for the Word of God itself. If you use them in addition to the Word, fine; but don't substitute just one Bible verse, plus an illustration, for the Scripture. Dig into the Word together, and have the family come up with their own illustrations and applications as you go.

GUIDELINE FIVE: *Include the memorization of*

Scripture. From the time a child is four or five, he's capable of memorizing verses which help guide the formation of character. In fact, most children can begin to commit short verses to memory even before they are of school age.

What should be committed to memory? Most parents begin with John 3:16, which is what Martin Luther called "The Gospel in a nutshell." But don't stop there. We have first taught our children some of the key passages that deal with salvation and the forgiveness of sin, such as Acts 16:31 which says, "Believe on the Lord Jesus Christ, and thou shalt be saved, and thy house"; and Romans 10:9 and 10:13; and I John 1:9.

We also learn verses that speak of God's guidance and care, such as Romans 8:28, Proverbs 3:5,6 and Psalms 23. Then we learn some "human relations" verses, such as Ephesians 4:32, which teaches that we must be kind to each other and forgive each other because God has forgiven us. As you introduce verses to be learned, be sure to lead an informal discussion of what each verse means to us today, and how we can learn to apply the verse in particular situations that may arise.

GUIDELINE SIX: *Learn to pray together.* Something happens when the members of a family join hands and look to God in prayer. I can't explain it. No one can measure it. But praying together has a way of bringing estranged members of a family together and lessening hurt and bitterness. It helps us to realize that we must forgive each other as God forgives us. Prayer should be as natural as breathing, but unlike breathing, a child has to be taught how to pray.

When families come together, what do they pray

about? Here are some suggestions:

Begin your time of prayer with thanksgiving. Learning to say "thank you," whether to members of the family or to our Heavenly Father, is a habit that must be cultivated. Remember Paul's words to the Philippians, ". . . In everything by prayer and supplication with thanksgiving let your requests be made know to God . . ." (Philippians 4:6).

It's easy for us to be completely selfish in our prayers: "God, give me this" and "Lord, give me that." This is one reason I object to the prayer that children are often taught:

Now I lay me down to sleep
I pray the Lord my soul to keep
If I should die before I wake
I pray the Lord my soul to take.

In that simple, four-line prayer, there are eight personal pronouns: *I, me,* or *my.* It's easy for us to become selfish in our prayer lives, so we need to cultivate the habit of saying, "Thank you, Father, for everything You have done."

Pray for your family needs. It's futile and unnecessary to pretend that everything is just fine when there are personal needs that affect your family. If there are financial needs in your home, make them a matter of family prayer, claiming Scriptures such as Philippians 4:19 together—where God promises to supply our needs according to His riches in glory.

Pray for each other's personal needs. James wrote to fellow Christians, "Pray for one another . . . ." Nowhere is this any more needed than in our homes where we live day by day.

When children disagree or can't get along, one may say, "We need to pray for more understanding and patience with one another." The mere admission of need for God's help enables Him to work in our lives. Pray for the father who is under stress, the child who is having difficulty in school, the child who is afraid of the dark at night.

Remember to pray for the leaders of our country. Paul wrote to Timothy, "First of all, then, I urge that entreaties and prayers, petitions and thanksgivings, be made on behalf of all men, for kings and all who are in authority, in order that we may lead a tranquil and quiet life in all godliness and dignity" (I Timothy 2:1,2, NASB).

In far too many homes, public officials are like sitting ducks at which everyone takes a shot. Everyone criticizes them. This is wrong. Respect for law and authority is taught as we pray for God to guide our leaders and use them

If you don't like what someone does, voice your feelings through proper channels, ones that have been particularly set up for redress, but don't create the feeling in your home that all public officials are simply targets for abuse. Paul instructed the Romans, "Let every person be in subjection to the governing authorities. For there is no authority except from God, and those which exist are established by God" (Romans 13:1, NASB). When the President or the governing officials of our country are under especially heavy pressure and stress, we join together as a family and pray for them.

Pray for the needs of fellow Christians. Never be guilty of just praying, "God bless us four and no more." When an article has appeared in a newspaper or publication concerning the persecution of Christians in a country where religious freedom is not allowed—and believe me, vast segments of the world's population are losing the freedom to worship according to the dictates of their own consciences—we read the article to our family as a reminder to pray for those fellow Christians.

If you can, pray for specific needs of believers. Pray for them by name, asking the Lord to meet particular needs.

Pray for Christian work at home and abroad. That includes your pastor and the leaders of your church, missionary families and Christian workers everywhere.

Have you ever heard someone pray, "God, bless all the missionaries everywhere"? I'm glad that they at least thought to mention "all the missionaries everywhere," but how much better to single out definite, particular needs!

A number of years ago our family began a plan which has encouraged our children to look beyond our personal concerns. We selected a number of missionary families and remembered just one in prayer daily, on a rotating basis. We asked the Lord to help them with adjustments to language, culture, homesickness, loneliness, differences of climate, personal adjustments, health, and anything else we could think of.

We have especially encouraged our children to pray for missionary children of the same age as they. A twelve-year-old knows something of the feelings of another twelve-year-old who perhaps may not be able to stay with parents, but is in a boarding home.

God does hear and answer prayer. You may want to do as we like to do in our family prayer, join hands and pray.

Pray as a family and you will learn that families

that pray together stay together—day after day and year after year.

The art of parenting is one which none of us will ever fully master. We're human. And in the process of guiding those little bundles from infancy to adulthood, we're bound to make many mistakes.

Fortunately, God doesn't expect us to be letter-perfect parents. That's why He is a loving, patient God who has promised His guidance for the task. Guidance through supernatural prompting, as we daily yield our wills to Him. And guidance through the principles in His Word, which we've examined throughout this book.

For us humans, the command to "Train up a child in the way he should go" is also followed by the reassuring promise: ". . . and when he is old, he will not depart from it." *That's* the joyful hope we have as parents. The promise direct from God that if we train up our children *His* way, all the effort will be well worth it.

It is my prayer for you that God will enrich your family life daily as you harness His guidelines for successful child-raising.

Notes

1. "His Life Is In Your Hands . . ."
1. "What's Happening to the American Family? *Better Homes and Gardens,* June, 1973, p. 4.

2. The Importance of the Early Years
1. Paul Wood, as quoted by S. I. McMillen, "How Are We Imprinting Our Children?" *Christian Life,* February, 1963, pp. 30-32.
2. James Dobson, as quoted by Richard Saltus, "Bucky Beaver' Can Ruin a Kid for Life, Doc Says," *Pacific Stars and Stripes,* September 1, 1974, p. 9.
3. McMillen, "How Are We Imprinting Our Children?" pp. 30-32.
4. Thomas Harris, *I'm OK—You're OK* (New York: Avon Books, 1973), pp. 43-44.

4. Learning to Communicate With Your Offspring
1. Larry Christenson, *The Christian Family* (Minneapolis: Bethany Fellowship, 1970), p. 177.

5. How to Discipline Effectively—God's Way
1. Ann Landers, "Say No to Your Children," *Reader's Digest,* October, 1968, p. 147.
2. Ibid, p. 146.
3. Dobson, *Dare to Discipline* (Wheaton, IL: Tyndale House, 1970), p. 18.
4. William Glasser, *Reality Therapy* (New York: Harper and Row, 1965), p. 16.
5. Haim Ginott, "How to Talk to Your Children," *Reader's Digest,* September, 1968, p. 79.
6. Glasser, *Reality Therapy,* p. 22.
7. Ginott, "How to Talk to Your Children," p. 79.

6. Conveying Values to Your Children
1. Fritz Ridenour, "What Christian Families Want to Know,"

Moody Monthly, November, 1974, p. 26.

2. Philip Yancey, "How Your Faith Affects Your Teenager," *Moody Monthly,* December, 1975, p. 56. Also see Merton Strommen's *Five Cries of Youth* (New York: Harper and Row, 1974).

3. Ibid, p. 56.

4. Howard Hendricks, *Heaven Help the Home!* (Wheaton, IL: Victor Books, 1974), pp. 20, 21.

5. Charles Ludwig, *Mama Was a Missionary* (Grand Rapids, MI: Zondervan Books, 1963), pp. 155, 156.

7. How to Tell Your Children About Sex

1. Lester Kirkendall, as quoted by Howard Hendricks in *Heaven Help the Home!* pp. 118, 119.

2. Wilson W. Grant, *From Parent to Child about Sex* (Grand Rapids, MI: Zondervan Books, 1973), pp. 92, 93.

3. Hendricks, *Heaven Help the Home!* p. 82.

8. How to Succeed With Your Teenager

1. Haim Ginott, *Between Parent and Teenager* (New York: Avon Books, 1971), pp. 23, 24

9. Making Family Worship Come Alive

1. Hendricks, *Heaven Help the Home!* pp. 87, 88.

2. Pitirim Sorokin, as quoted by Tim LaHaye, *How to Be Happy Though Married* (Wheaton, IL: Tyndale House Publishers, 1972), p. 49.

TRAIN UP A CHILD
AND BE GLAD YOU DID

BEING A PARENT is one of the last hold-outs of the amateurs! To drive a car, operate a CB radio, be a plumber, or practice medicine, you must be licensed—indicating that you have a certain level of training and expertise in performing that function. But when it comes to being a parent, no professional training or experience is required. It's easy to become a parent, but hard to parent. If you are about ready to cry "Help!" look here for answers. Better yet, read this book with a prayer that you will be kept from making grave mistakes in parenting.

A WELL-KNOWN VOICE on radio, Dr. Sala heads Guidelines, Inc., an international ministry directed to 30 countries of the world. His two radio programs, "Guidelines—A Five-Minute Commentary" and "Guidelines for Family Living," are released 800 times weekly in 15 English-speaking countries and are translated into 12 languages. Guidelines, Inc., also produces Christian literature in various languages. Father of three children, the author and his family make their home in Mission Viejo, California.

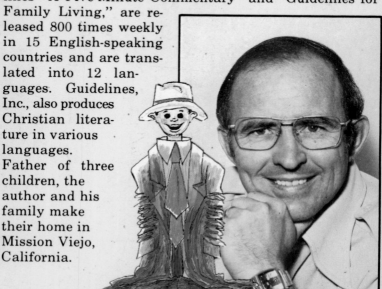

ISBN 0-916406-95-4

AC-1048 395